Garland Studies in

COMPARATIVE LITERATURE

GENERAL EDITOR
James J. Wilhelm
Rutgers University

ASSOCIATE EDITOR
Richard Saez
College of Staten Island, C.U.N.Y.

A GARLAND SERIES

WORDS HEARD AND OVERHEARD
THE MAIN TEXT IN CONTEMPORARY DRAMA

Robert F. Gross

GARLAND PUBLISHING
New York & London
1990

Copyright © 1990 by Robert F. Gross
All Rights Reserved

Library of Congress Cataloging-in-Publication Data

Gross, Robert F.
Words heard and overheard: the main text in contemporary drama/ Robert F. Gross
p. cm.—(Garland studies in comparative literature)
Includes bibliographical references.
ISBN 0-8240-5573-X (alk. paper)
1.Drama—20th century—History and criticism. 2. Style, Literary.
I. Title. II. Series.
PN1861.G65   1990
809.2'04—dc20   90-40752

Printed on acid-free, 250-year-life paper.
Manufactured in the United States of America

CONTENTS

Preface vii
Acknowledgments ix
Introduction x
Critical Considerations 1
Running out of Words:
   Inadmissible Evidence 29
The Silent Retreat:
   Bingo 57
Hearing a Name:
   Véra Baxter 77
Strange Music:
   The Hunting Party 95
Fragments of the Inexpressible:
   The Irrational Are Dying Out 119
Vamping with Dad:
   A Prelude to Death in Venice 139
Conclusion 153
Works Cited 161

PREFACE

The following study sets out to explore some of the distinguishing features of dramatic literature. It does so through the close reading of six dramatic texts as aesthetic objects. Although this approach may be regarded as hopelessly quaint in certain circles, especially those of the cultural materialists, who prefer to see texts as products caught up in the interplay of institutional interests, I believe that the careful reading of individual texts comes closest to the process of interpretation most needed by those who actually work in the theatre. For, despite all the insight that can be gained from sociological approaches toward the theatre as an institution (and they are many), the actor, the director, the designer and the dramaturg ultimately must function on a far more minute level if they are to do their work well. The importance of a word, a pause, the timing of an entrance, the reason why one piece of information is introduced before another--this is how a play is produced, and it is through that accumulation of countless details that we as an audience are delighted or moved, electrified or bored. The current enthusiasm for critical theory is only helpful in the theatre when it does not take so Olympian a viewpoint that it obscures the unique details that are the stuff of theatre, and the manifold relationships that gives it power.

ACKNOWLEDGMENTS

This project, which began over a decade ago as a doctoral dissertation, and has now emerges in a very different form indeed after many years, has had the benefit of much apppreciaiton, questioning, and support. As a graduate student in Comparative Literature at the University of North Carolina-Chapel Hill, I benefited enormously from the encouragement, intellectual stimulation, and guidance of Professors Kimball King and Graydon Ekdal. Professor Eugene Falk deserves special thanks for his patience in dealing with the theoretical presuppositions of the dissertation in such detail.

Between the dissertation and the book, there have been many productions, many courses, and many other projects. The intervening time has been enriched by countless conversations and critical disputes, too many to be remembered, let alone acknowledged. Yet three conversations have continued with particular persistence and value over the past decade, and have helped me particularly in the process of rethinking this book--conversations with Tom Haas, Stephanie Barbé Hammer, and Ralph Dressler. I look forward to those conversations continuing in the decades to come. Jim Gulledge has been of inestimable help, not only in the preparation of this manuscript, and initiating me to the mysteries of Nota Bene software (which was used for text processing and page layout of this manuscript), but in more ways than he can ever know. To him goes a very special thanks.

And throughout both dissertation and book, my Mother, my six remarkable and beloved siblings, and the all the varied and marvelous spouses and children they have collected along the way, have been constant sources of encouragement and support.

Hobart and William Smith Colleges are to be thanked for both financial support in the preparation of the manuscript, and for a leave that made it possible. Many thanks to Acting Provost Tamar March for her help in these matters, and for her commitment to making sure my scholarship did not perish under the *Angst* of too many theatrical crises at the Colleges.

INTRODUCTION

The "talked-to-death trinity" [totgesagte Trinität] (Lehrman 1973) of literary criticism--drama, lyric, and narrative--still proves to be one of the most tenacious sets of literary classification. Suggested by the Platonic distinction between mimetic and diegetic kinds of literature in Book 3 of *The Republic* and by Aristotle's tripartite division in Chapter 3 of the *Poetics*, the classification was adapted and elaborated by German Romantic critics, and has demanded the attention of literary scholars to this day. Of the three kinds, drama proclaims its uniqueness most clearly, since it alone finds its fulfillment on the boards rather than in the study. At the same time, drama differs from other forms of theatre, such as dance and pantomime, since it includes spoken language among the means of artistic representation appropriate to it. Related to both the arts of performance and the art of literature, dramatic kind has posed special problems of critical method and has led to a general uneasiness that can be perceived in most theories of drama. Certain modern theorists, represented by Antonin Artaud in his most extreme pronouncements, have repudiated the literary aspects of theatre entirely, while more literary minds, such as Jiří Veltruský's (Matejka & Titunik 1976, 95), have suggested that a dramatic text can be legitimately considered without reference to theatrical performance. Neither extreme can do full justice to the complexities of drama.

Definitions of drama that ignore the theatrical *telos* of the dramatic text tend to focus on arbitrary criteria. In *Irony and Drama*, Bert O. States (1971) argues that the literary kind "drama" is completely independent of "theatre," that is, performance, and defines drama as a dialectical form that requires the presence of ironic reversals of action. States, a proponent of Kenneth Burke's "dramatistic" theories, relates the dramatic to a mode of thought that structures reality dialectically. In a dramatic plot, States explains, every action leads inevitably to its opposite, and irony is the mode most appropriate to drama because irony uses an assertion to express its opposite. Such extensive reliance on irony and peripety blurs the distinction between genre and mode. Following States' argument, one could conclude that Evelyn Waugh's *Vile Bodies* is a novel and *Play*, a drama. Identifying the essential characteristic of drama on the level of incident, *Irony and Drama* presents a classification of plot structure rather than of kind. The plot of *Madame Bovary* is certainly far more heavily ironic than the Chester Corpus Christi plays, but it does not serve the cause of critical clarity to call a novel more "dramatic" than a play, when the observation "more ironic" would be more germane. Although critics as different as William Archer (1913, 23-31), Gustav Freytag (1968, 104-105), and Bertolt Brecht (1967, 936-937), have pointed out he dramatic value of conflict, none of them have stated that drama is synonymous with irony and dialectic.

Emil Staiger (1956, 143-171) makes a similar error, although he chooses *anagnorisis* as his defining principle instead of *peripeteia*. The interaction of "pathos" and "problem" define the kind, a structure of events motivated by emotional intensity and leading to the unfolding of a situation. Drama exposes the foundation [*Worumwillen*] of any situation and reveals the fundamental interdependence among all of its events. Although such a definition of drama illuminates the Classical tradition, from *Oresteia* to *Phèdre* and *Rosmersholm*, it fails to explain the dramatic qualities of *Danton's Death*, *Uncle Vanya*, or *The Caretaker*. It is more profitable to follow the examples of Plato and Aristotle, who differentiated among kinds by their essential means of presentation rather than by contingent qualities of plot structure. Neither States' reversal nor Staiger's recognition are dramatic constant.

I have chosen to analyze drama through the distinct functions of language in that literary kind. The approach is hardly new; it can be found in the *Poetics*. It is a clear and obvious place to begin, since the division of speech between actors clearly differentiates the form from either lyric poetry or epic. This is not to say that there are no generic hybrids; merely that those fascinating oddities will not be the subject of observation here.

Introduction

Although the functions of dramatic speech have become a major topic of inquiry over the past generation, many questions remain unanswered, due in large part to the methodological weaknesses of most studies dealing with the topic. Anglo-American critics of drama have addressed themselves to two sets of questions. First, what have been the effects of realistic conventions on stage speech, and what limitations does realistic speech impose on modern attempts to write tragedy? *The Language of Tragedy* (Prior 1947) *The Frontiers of Drama* (Ellis-Fermor 1964) represent the two most sophisticated treatments of these questions to date. The second question concerns the experiments of Beckett, Pinter, Ionesco, and the early Albee, asks how contemporary writers are able to use the debased and devalued language of modern life, the victim of demagogues and advertising agencies, to create significant works of art. *The Theatre of the Absurd* (Esslin 1961) has been the most influential and popular treatment of this question. Both approaches have been limited by the absence of a clear definition of the nature of dramatic speech. Unexamined critical presuppositions greatly limit the usefulness of the only two extended studies of language in contemporary British drama, *Theatre Language* (Brown 1972) and *Six Dramatists in Search of a Language* (Kennedy 1975), both of which exhibit a certain critical naivete concerning their own methods.

Some studies of individual playwrights follow more rigorous approaches. *Shaw: The Style and the Man* (Ohmann 1962) begins with a promising foray into stylistics, but soon becomes lost in the doldrums of psycho-biographical speculations. *Samuel Beckett's Dramatic Language* (Eliopulos 1975) can be praised as a consistent application of a rhetorical approach, but the study fails to offer more than a descriptive listing of Beckett's major dramatic devices. *The Pinter Problem* (Quigley 1975) is a stimulating attempt to apply insights from Wittgenstein to Pinter's dramatic conundrums, but the application of Wittgenstein's observations on language games to the relationships between Pinter's characters does not pay sufficient attention to the functions of dramatic language in relationship to the spectator. Dealing primarily with the ways in which language defines and reveals the dynamics of interpersonal relationships in daily life, Quigley does not place Wittgenstein's ideas in a literary context, but deals with dramatic characters as if they were real people.

A survey of the highlights of Continental criticism on the topic of dramatic speech is somewhat more rewarding. Here, one again finds many studies of dubious value, such as *Geschlossene und Offene Form im Drama* (Klotz 1969) and *Sprache und Dramaturgie* (Blank 1969), both of which establish two contrasting models of dramatic structure and language. Resembling those epigrams that begin "There are two kind of people...," these studies are more striking than true, since the great mass of dramatic literature falls between the two, somewhat arbitrarily selected, dramatic models. The single most enlightening essay, "Functions of Language in the Theater" (Ingarden 1973 *Literary Work*, 377-396) as well as various essays by Jiří Veltruský and Jan Mukařovský, are valuable, though their approaches are more theoretical than critical, and demand the test of application. *The Semiotics of Theatre and Drama* (Elam 1980) brings much of this material together with the best of Italian semiotic criticism in what remains the best general volume on theatrical semiotics in English. A far less rigorous attempt to bring semiotic theory to bear on theatre, *The Field of Drama* (Esslin 1987), moves far too quickly over far too much terrain to be of much value. Hermeneutic theorist Hans-Georg Gadamer (1975) offers useful insights but requires particularly careful interpretation, since he is not directly concerned with the nature of dramatic speech. He is far more interested in defining a model of understanding, than developing a theatrical aesthetics.

There is a great need for all of this critical material to be collected, compared, applied, and evaluated. Obviously, no single study can hope to do justice to the question of dramatic language in its full complexity and variety, let along deal with all the major theories as well. This study will deal with a few of the questions as they relate to the problems posed by representative plays written by six major contemporary dramatists --John Osborne's *Inadmissible Evidence*, Edward Bond's *Bingo*, Marguerite Duras' *Véra Baxter*, Thomas Bernhard's *The Hunting Party*, Peter Handke's *The Irrational Are Dying Out* and Lee Breuer's *A Prelude to Death in Venice*. Even though the plays differ substantially in style, one could still rightly object that they represent only a small segment of the entire spectrum of dramatic literature, from Kalidasa to the latest postmodern monologist. I freely admit the limitation, since I am constructing a model for analytical purposes, a model that will vary in its applications to the six texts, and does not mean to provide a general method for the analysis of all works of dramatic literature. They provide six distinctive occasions against which to test the validity of the conclusions arrived at in the opening chapter.

Each play will provide an opportunity for particular problems of description and interpretation. *Inadmissible Evidence* is dominated by the isolated figure of its protagonist, whose vision of his personal dilemma remains essentially unchanged despite his heated exchanges with the other characters. The lack of dialectical development between the characters challenges certain definitions of dramatic development. In *Bingo*, the inability of the characters to establish and maintain an ongoing relationship through speech gives rise to a series of monologic assertions that create static constellations of meaning rather than dialectical development. *Véra Baxter* is a tale of enigmatic encounters, in which the opacity of the characters and their emotional states becomes central. The language suggests, only to deny or evade, the matters at hand. *The Hunting Party* shows us characters who are locked into obsessive patterns, and the obsessions are presented through language that is highly mannered and lacking individual expression. The characters' speeches are often asserted against the silence, rather than against the other speeches. Here, drama is moving toward the condition of a lyric poem. *The Irrational Are Dying out* establishes two modes of speech, corresponding to two views of reality, and investigates the impossibility of maintaining communication between the two. The contrast between the two languages, one clear and the other increasingly enigmatic, generates a movement into obscurity. In *A Prelude to Death in Venice*, the voices and figures function as part of a single psyche, and the play progresses, not through the interaction of characters, but through the revision of mythic material.

CRITICAL CONSIDERATIONS

Speech in the Theatre

Drama can most easily be recognized on the page by the alternation of main text [*Haupttext*] and side text [*Nebentext*] (Ingarden 1973 *Literary Work* , 208-9). The main text is composed of all of the lines spoken by characters within the world presented by the play. The main text is almost always accompanied by a side text that serves as a major indication that the work is a drama. The side text is composed of all those statements not uttered by the characters; stage directions and the attributions of speeches in the main text to their speakers are the most common examples of side text. In performance, the side text disappears as a linguistic formation, and the stage directions are presented through the actions of the actors, lighting and sound effects, costumes and scenery. Unlike the narrative and lyric, which create their presented worlds totally through language, a theatrical performance creates a world through a mixture of language and real objects. Thus, the means of theatrical presentation, being distinct from the means of narrative and lyric, radically affect the role of description in drama, as opposed to other literary kinds. Sophocles does not describe Kreon's physical appearance, nor does Shakespeare describe Macbeth's, but the novelist Henry James describes the physical appearance of his protagonist in *The American*, Christopher Newman, at great length. Despite that fact, however, Newman will remain a complex of schematic statements on the printed page, relying on the imaginational acts of the reader to complete his portrait, while Macbeth will be represented in performance by an actor whose appearance will leave no question of height, weight, posture, complexion, etc., undetermined. Macbeth, unlike Newman, will be represented by an actor, an autonomous real being whose appearance will not be dependent upon the imaginational acts of a spectator. Physical description, therefore, plays a much greater role in narrative literature; in the main text of a stage play it is usually either redundant or theatrically ineffective.

In purely descriptive narration the narrator is self-effacing; he stands outside of the imaginary world presented by the text and projects a series of statements around that world. Consider, for example, the opening sentences of a "pure" third person narrative, *The American*:

> On a brilliant day in May, in the year 1868, a gentleman was reclining at his ease on the great circular divan which at that period occupied the centre of the Salon Carré, in the Museum of the Louvre. This commodious ottoman has since been removed, to the extreme regret of all weak-kneed lovers of the fine arts; but the gentleman in question had taken serene possession of its softest spot, and, with his head thrown back and his legs outstretched, was staring at Murillo's beautiful moon-borne Madonna in profound enjoyment of his posture. He had removed his hat, and flung beside him a little red guide-book and an opera-glass (James 1983, 515).

The narrator of this passage cannot be considered a literary character, although "he" has an identifiable style, tone, and point of view. The sentences create the scene presented to the reader's imagination, and the world exists only through those sentences projected by that narrator. He stands outside of that ontic sphere which he projects, and there is no way to move beyond James' narrator and establish him within the presented world of *The American*. It is equally impossible to question whether his account of the story is correct or not. We see that he is superior to the presented world in several ways: he is temporally superior to the world when he relates the fortunes of the ottoman since May, 1868; he is spatially superior to it, because he is able to "move" within the gallery and focus on details without having to cope with the restrictions of a physical body; he is intellectually superior, since he can tell how Newman enjoys his posture without telling us how this information was procured. He is equally disinterested and disembodied. The reader is not led to consider the motivations that have led to the composition of this literary description. The statements exist independently of any individualized speaker.

The speeches in the main text of a drama, on the other hand, are all actions performed by characters within the presented world of the play. Although Winnie in Beckett's *Happy Days* has virtually all the lines in the main text of that play, she still does not create the world of the play in the way that James' narrator does. Winnie's very existence is the result of the projections of an anonymous presenter far more elusive and self-effacing than James' narrator, one who presents the world within Winnie and her husband exist. The speeches of Osborne's characters are the *presented* text, since these speeches exist as actions that are performed by figures within the presented world of the play. Those presented actions obviously cannot project themselves; Winnie cannot project herself and the world of *Happy Days* . The presented text requires a *presentative* text that lies outside of the created ontic realm (Falk 1981, 69-71). This dramatic presentative text serves a similar function to that of the narration in *The American*. The clearest evidence of the presentative text is found in the side text, in those anonymously projected assertions that reveal the presence of a superior artificer behind this presented world:

> MRS. DUDEBAT: (*sitting down and breaking down*) Oh, you none of you care. You see people die every day.
> RIDGEON: (*petting her*) Nonsense! it's nothing: I told him to come in and say that, I thought I should want to get rid of you.
> MRS. DUDEBAT: (*shocked at the falsehood*) Oh!
> RIDGEON: (*continuing*) Don't look so bewildered: there's nobody dying.
> MRS. DUDEBAT: My husband is.
> RIDGEON: (*pulling himself together*) Ah, yes: I had forgotten your husband. (Shaw 1954, 122)

With virtually every line in this passage, Shaw makes his presence felt, whether adding blocking, explaining motive, or clarifying the links between lines. Shaw develops his presentative text more than most dramatists, even giving us lengthy descriptions and narrative passages, which keep us aware of his presence. (The famous Shavian preface might be seen as side text run amok.)

Since dramatic characters are not autonomous and are therefore incapable of creating their own speeches, their "presented" speeches are projected by the presentative text as well as by themselves. Thus, every speech in the main text is projected twice; first, by the anonymous narrator, and, secondly, by the character. In performance, however, the presence of the presentative text is minimized; the spectator only hears the voices of the actors speaking the main text, and not the silent, implicit voice of the presenter. The presence of that presenter in the side text vanishes into the *mise en scène*, into the blocking, and into the acting, thus strengthening the spectator's illusion that the figures onstage are autonomous figures within the world of the play. Shaw's presenter, unlike James' narrator, cannot interrupt the ongoing action to explain the significance of a single element ihn the continually unfolding spectacle; the characters' presented actions must establish their meaning without the aid of direct authorial commentary.

Most of the speeches in the main text of a drama are spoken by one character to another. In most realistic dramas, such as Ibsen's *Ghosts*, every speech is addressed to an onstage interlocutor, while in more presentational dramas, such as Aristophanes' *The Clouds*, the spectator is addressed directly. Even if the dramatist attempts to establish the illusion of a self-contained presented world, whose characters are totally unaware of the spectator's presence, the world behind the proscenium arch is not totally closed in upon itself. The presented world always presents itself to a spectator. This spectator is not any particular audience with its unique prejudices, whims, and expectations, nor is it an amalgam of all possible audiences. It is a hypothetical spectator implicit in the aesthetic nature of the drama itself (Ingarden 1973 *Literary Work*, 232). It is necessary to accept the implicit presence of the spectator for whom the play is presented, since the actors, insofar as they are involved in the various tasks required to present the world, are unable to achieve a complete apprehension of all the aesthetic values of the production. They are working within the play, not witnessing it. The act of presentation, in order to find its completion, must be presented to a spectator who can observe all of the aesthetic aspects as they are presented.

Every speech is presented for the spectator, though it is usually addressed to an onstage interlocutor as well. As a result, a speech may have one meaning within the presented world of the play, in which the characters--speaker and interlocutor--have only a partial understanding of their world and are too immersed in their own actions to be able to perceive the complete implications of their speeches, and another meaning for the spectator, who can see the entire presented world unfolding before him. The difference between these two simultaneous presentations varies in degree, but it is always present. The disparity is most obvious in cases of dramatic irony, which creates effects through the gap between what the speaker intends by his/her utterance and what the spectator understands by it, having access to the entire verbal structure while the speaker and onstage interlocutors have only partial access, and, as a result, perceive a meaning quite different from what the spectator perceives. When Oedipus says to Kreon, "By avenging Laios' death, I protect myself" (Sophocles 1978, ll.171), neither he or Kreon perceive an irony. Indeed, for a member of the audience who does not know the whole story of Oedipus, the line carries no irony. Only the spectator who knows that Oedipus is the murderer of Laios experiences an ironic recognition there. Every speech in a play must be understood both as an utterance within the presented world of the play, and as an utterance that pierces through the limits of that presented world to reach the spectator (Ingarden 1973 *Literary Work*, 394-95).

Because each speech in the main text is articulated by a character within the text's presented world, it takes on the nature of an action. The opening description in *The American* is not enacted by anyone; it appears to exist independently of any particularized and motivated act of meaning. The description provides information about the scene without contributing to a portrait of the narrator as an active figure within the presented realm of the text. In a play, each speech is delivered by a character, simultaneously providing information about the scene and about the speaker. The attitude of the speaker toward the topic, the attitude of the speaker toward the interlocutor, and the general mood of the speaker is as important as the topic under discussion. In narrative, the language gives the impression of having been "completed"; we can open the book to any passage and begin to read. The actions exist in a fictional past, and the whole artifact refers to a completed action. In the main text of a drama, the speeches are presented as actions in the present tense; they seem to be formed before our very eyes, without the temporal interval that separates the reader of narrative from the imagined event. Dramatic speech is presented as present action.

To realize the implications of the dramatic presentation of language as action, it is first necessary to consider the processes underlying our speech acts in everyday life. In Edmund Husserl's *Logical Investigation*, he defines the various aspects of speech. That complex analysis, going far beyond our purposes here both in depth and complexity, provides a basic understanding of speech necessary for any investigation of dramatic speech.

Each expression, Husserl explains, is the result of two actions; a prelinguistic judgment or impulse, and an action in which the phonic material is endowed with meaning, and is thus constituted as a sign. Together, the phonic material and the endowed meaning constitute a word that is intersubjectively given. The statement is a projection of the speaker's intentional act of understanding towards an interlocutor. It sets forth a state of affairs [*Sachverhalt*]. It is through a series of assertions that Henry James establishes an unfolding of states of affairs at the beginning of *The American*: the day in May, the gentleman on the ottoman at the Louvre, his posture, and so forth. Any written text, from a news story to a recipe, asserts a series of statements that constitute changing states of affairs within its presented world. The functions of these expressions, as Ingarden demonstrated in detail in *The Literary Work of Art*, are put to distinctive ends in works of literature.

But a speaking subject projects more than just a state of affairs through an expression. The speaker not only projects a state of affairs, but secondarily communicates information about him/herself as well. One's countenance, inflections, gestures, and bearing, as well as word choice and order, inform the interlocutor about the psychic state of the speaker, including his/her attitudes both toward the expression's object and the situation in which the statement is made. These actions always accompany the speaker's act of meaning, although they are not moments of the meaning itself:

Speech in the Theatre

Such 'utterances' are not expressions in the sense in which a case of speech is an expression, they are not phenomenally one with the experience made manifest in them in the consciousness of the man who manifests them, as in the case with speech (Husserl 1970, I:275).

Although these acts are not expressions, they indicate the presence of certain psychic states. They are not meaningful signs, which are bound to their meaning by a conventional definition, but they are more accurately described as *indications*, in the way that the symptoms of a disease might "indicate" the presence of a disease rather than stand as a meaningful sign for that disease. These intimated, or, as Ingarden calls them, *manifestative qualities*, [*Kundgabefunktionen*] (1973 *Literary Work*, 60) do not carry lexical meaning. "To understand an intimation is not to have conceptual knowledge of it," writes Husserl (1970, I:277). A sigh, a raised eyebrow, a shrug of the shoulders do not have meaning and, therefore, need to be interpreted in reference to its context. Isolated from its context, it is virtually impossible to determine what a specific gesture might indicate.

Each expression manifests information on two levels. On the more general level, it indicates the simple desire of the speaker to communicate meaning. On the more specific level, the emotional coloring of the speech may reveal attitudes and emotional states. Every speech is motivated; that is, it finds its origin in a psychic act that lies behind the speech. The manifestative qualities may give the listener important indications about the speaker, in addition to the states of affairs projected by the speaker.

Can this model of speech, drawn from observation of life, be applied to drama, or would that transposition be an unwitting lapse into näive realism, assuming that the rules of life must apply to art? An answer to this question is suggested by a passage in Husserl's *Cartesian Meditations*. In the fifth Meditation, Husserl defends his phenomenological theory from charges of solipsism by explaining how the individual ego is able to perceive others as autonomous centers of consciousness (Husserl 1960, 89-90). Although the ego experiences itself in the spatial mode "here", existing within its own body, and views others externally in the spatial mode "there", it becomes aware that those other figures perceive themselves in a manner essentially identical to the way in which the ego perceives itself, i. e. , in its unique awareness of its physical being and its awareness of its own "hereness" The ego comes to this conclusion through acts of imaginative empathy, or *pairing*. Through pairing, the ego first realizes that the body which it experiences in the spatial mode "there" experiences itself in the spatial mode "here". The subsequent actions of the other person reinforces this initial experience of that consciousness. Husserl observes:

> Regarding experience of someone else, it is clear that its fulfillingly verifying continuation can ensue *only by means of appresentations that* proceed in a synthetically harmonious fashion. (1960, 89-90)

When I listen to someone speak, I cannot directly apprehend the prelinguistic act that founds each expression. I hear only a linguistic formulation, but become aware of its meaning and prelinguistic foundation by means of my analogous act of meaning, in which I confer meaning on the phonic material I hear, and constitute a state of affairs that has been evoked by that expression. Through acts of pairing, I conclude that the sounds I hear are the result of an act of meaning essentially identical to my own. This is not to say that I necessarily project my personal motivations and mental quirks on the speaker, but only that I become aware that his expression is an act of meaning motivated by certain impulses and brought about by certain psychic acts. The impulses and psychic acts cannot be directly apprehended, but, like the side of a sphere not immediately accessible to my vision, those impulses and acts are co-given with the linguistic act. Acts of pairing are virtually unconscious and automatic, and I do not hesitate to assume that those I see before me in human form possess the same intentionality that I possess.

Because I assume the co-giveness of corresponding psychic acts when I hear someone speak, I carry that assumption into my experience of drama, and assume the same co-giveness present in those expressions that compose the main text of a play. The playwright generally relies on my unconscious tendency to pair when s/he creates the illusion that the characters are autonomous centers of consciousness within the presented world. The playwright who violates the illusion that each speech presupposes a psychic act disorients the spectator, whose immediate and unconscious presuppositions, founded on daily experience, are suddenly undermined. With the language of the main text no longer fostering the illusion that it is founded in prelinguistic acts of the characters but is imposed on the speaking figures by another consciousness (that is, the playwright's), the main text loses the illusion of being produced within the presented world. We can now see the ventriloquist, and notice his/her lips begin to move.

Traditionally, this dissociation of character and speech serves the ends of parody, and there is a tradition of dramatic burlesque, ranging from Shakespeare's *A Midsummer Night's Dream* to Stoppard's *The Real Inspector Hound* which capitalizes on the potential humor implicit in all bad drama, which calls attention to the unskilled hand of a poor dramatist making hash of the presented world. This technique has been appropriated by some modern dramatists for satiric purposes, as in Tzara's *The Gas Heart* and Ionesco's *The Bald Soprano*, foregoing the framing devices used by more traditional dramatists to set off their parodies. The disruption of the pairing function, however, produces only the most superficial and limited range of comic devices, and is thus useful by itself only in playlets. Even *The Bald Soprano*, the most consistently delightful of these sustained anti-pairing plays, easily profits in production by judicious pruning. The disruption of pairing, if it is to achieve any depth or insight, seems to require a frame in which pairing, and the greater emotional and imaginative possibilities that accompany it, can be developed.

The effect of the pairing function is strengthened in production, because the spectator no longer reads lines that are merely attributed to a character in the text, but sees and hears those lines delivered by an actor whose physical presence represents the autonomous center of the character's consciousness. It is the presence of a human body onstage which more strongly compels acts of pairing from the spectator. Inept actors tend to unconsciously undermine the spectator's natural tendency to pair. For example, one of the most damning criticisms that can be made about a performance is that it sounded as if the actor had recited the lines by rote, instead of appearing to confer meaning on the sounds s/he uttered. In obviously mechanical recitations, the manifestative qualities are drastically reduced, and the words seem to be little more than phonic material, without meaning or prelinguistic founding:

> To recite is the contrary of speaking. Recitation knows what is coming and is closed to the sudden idea. All of us have

had the experience of listening to a bad actor and getting the impression when he said one word he was already thinking of the next. This is not speaking. (Gadamer 1975, 497)

The actor's task is to re-endow the phonic material with meaning, leading us to infer the existence of prelinguistic acts behind it.

In a style far removed from the highly specialized, conceptual style of phenomenological aesthetics, theatrical directors and have written about the expressive qualities of the main text, and the problems of realizing them in performance. Sir Tyrone Guthrie put it this way:

> Where I think the producer's work of coordination requires the greatest amount of time and care spent upon it is in the vocal interpretation of the play. As I have already tried to indicate, the performance of a play is, on a smaller scale, a performance of a musical work. The script is, as it were, sung, because speaking and singing are, after all, the same process. Although I am speaking now and not singing, I am uttering a definable tune all the time. Every sentence that I phrase is consciously phrased in a certain rhythm. The pauses, although I am not conscious of it, are expressing an instinctive need to pause, not merely to breathe, but for clarity and various other interpretative purposes. This is even more pronounced in the performance of a play, where all that has been most carefully thought out in terms of pace, rhythm, pitch, volume and all the rest of it, to make a certain expressive effect. (1967, 374-375)

Guthrie discusses the interpretation of the main text as if it were a musical score, and the production process the shaping of the words in such a way as to maximize the expressive qualities of the language. Rather than beginning with a reconstruction of the prelinguistic states, he works to heighten the dynamics used by speakers in everyday conversation.

Konstantin Stanislavski writes from a very different working orientation than Guthrie, and his similarities to Husserl are even greater. For him, the actor must begin with the main text, and then go back to construe the extralinguistic context and the prelinguistic judgments implied by the words. Husserl's theoretical observation that every expression is founded in a prelinguistic judgment finds its practical counterpart in Stanislavksi's "Whatever happens onstage must be for a *purpose*"(1936, 33). The spoken word is the physical component of a psychophysical action for Stanislavski as well as for Husserl, and manifestative qualities emerge most vividly for the well-trained Stanislavskian actor concentrates on the immediate actions of his/her character, remembering the given circumstances and objectives, instead of diverting his/her attention to arbitrary movements, technical gimmicks, and clichès of emotion (Moore 1965, 58-61).

Although Jerzy Grotowski has been heavily influenced by the theories of Artaud and shares few opinions with Stanislavski, he does agree that all stage speech is action founded in the psychic states of the characters:

> You must be conscious of the action founded behind the works... Almost always the deeper meaning of our reaction is hidden. (Grotowski 1968, 235)

The actor must play the present action; this is the belief shared by all major theoreticians of acting in the Western tradition, whether disciples of Artaud, Stanislavski, or Brecht. The actor must deliver his lines in accordance with his own intentions, instead of merely mouthing a sequence of memorized sounds.

The idea of a dramatic character is not directly represented, but emerges from the sequence of actions performed by the actor playing the character. An actor cannot represent those qualities that constitute Richard III. He must enact Richard's cynical reflections, his audacious wooing of Lady Anne, his dismissal of Buckingham, as well as his other actions, and allow the constituitive qualities to emerge from those actions. The actor who decides to play the abstract quality of villainy throughout the performance will produce a monotonous and ineffective Richard. An actor must not allow his preconceived notion of the character to dominate the varied action presented in the text.

When a drama is properly actualized in production, it is enhanced by the addition of manifestative qualities that are far deeper and more subtle than those merely suggested in the text. A spectator who is present at a good performance of *Rosmersholm*, *Medea*, or *King Lear* confronts the immediate presence of powerful emotion in a way unknown to a reader of those plays. The greater emotional intensity of a performance is to a great extent the result of the actor's physical presence onstage, which allows manifestative qualities to emerge through physical actions that could only be expressed in a written text through the medium of words. The signifying aspects of human behavior are heightened in the theatre; "a good actor will probably exaggerate just that part of the entire pattern that has the highest communicative value" (Stern 1973, 120).

The emotional intensity of performance is further heightened by the fact that the audience and actors share a common time and place of performance, making the presented world physically tangible and present to the senses of the audience. Within that space, the spectator is able to view an entire array of emotional states, simultaneously arising from the various onstage characters, developing according to different rhythm and tempi. The novelist must present simultaneity through a linear sequence of descriptive statements, which the reader must mentally constitute into a tableau in a series of discrete acts of meaning. The theatrical spectator, on the other hand, is immediately confronted by a tableau, in which several things may be happening simultaneously. Although a speaking character's words may tend to pull focus, emphasizing that character's psychic state, indications of emotion are also being communicated by the silent characters onstage, interacting with the speaker, and modifying our vision of the entire *Gestalt*. Those pieces of behavior, whether spoken or silent, that most strongly manifest the psychic lives of the characters tend to dominate the stage.

For these reasons, the drama is perhaps the most passionate of all literary forms, or, at least, the one whose stock in trade has most consistently been the representation of intense passions; Prometheus, Othello, Volpone, Phèdre, Marguerite Gautier, Claire Zachanassian--the great roles of the theatre, taken together, express the full range of human passion, in its most heightened and acute forms. Even Chekhov's understated portraits manifest deep emotions powerfully--Masha and Mme. Ranevskaya are no less intense for their subtlety and indirection. And even that supposed master of detachment, Bertolt Brecht, certainly did not shy away from the passions when he drew Shen Te, Galileo, and Mother Courage.

An emotion, like the idea of a character, cannot be presented to us in abstract terms. It must be manifested through the actions of a character. These emotions emerge in the moment-to-moment unfolding of a dramatic situation as present action. Each expression is as an action performed by a character, which points simultaneously back toward the already vanishing context that is being altered by the expression, down to the prelinguistic state that is manifested in the expression, and forward toward the future effect it might have on the situation. The present action is the vehicle which makes it possible for the spectator to simultaneously infer the past impulse and anticipate the future effect, while experiencing the present act of meaning. In a good production, we are given a heightened awareness of the significance of each moment of behavior, allowing us to intuit as an essential unity the aspects of that moment.

The dramatic importance of emotion it its unfolding led Roman Ingarden to observe that unemotional disinterested speeches are not theatrically effective, and that good dramatic speech is motivated by desires that shape the course of the action and are manifested in the main text (Ingarden 1973 *Literary Work*, 386-390). This "active" discourse is the fundamental mode of dramatic speech. This explains why Plato's *Phaedrus* and John Dryden's *Essay of Dramatic Poesy*, although written conversational form, with side text and main text, do not strike readers as inherently dramatic. In both cases, the language is self-sufficient to the didactic end of the work; it does not require actors to strengthen the few coincidental manifestative qualities that the text might indicate. Or, to express the same observation in Stanislavskian terms, these texts lack subtexts. When manifestative qualities are of little importance, there is no need for a theatrical performance to "complete" the work. The truly dramatic text, on the other hand, finds its fulfillment in production.

Since the main text always refers back to an implicit subtext, we are repeatedly drawn to the prelinguistic act implicit in ever expression. We are drawn from the expression to what it indicates, from definable words on the page to vague stirrings within the soul. This repeated movement toward the implicit causes difficulties in the critical interpretation of dramatic texts. The critic cannot state the prelinguistic impulse in its particularity, but can only infer a possible range of valid emotional states from the situation and the expressions. As Husserl (1970, I:277) stated, the perception of manifestative qualities depends on intuition rather than conceptual thought. Since the impulse evades rigid definition, a number of different interpretations of the same role may be equally valid and justified by the text.

There is, however, a limited range of valid interpretations, established by the states of affairs within the text, and these are the marks by which productions are mounted and judged. Mary Tyrone cannot be played with the blithe flirtatiousness of Lorelei Lee, nor Uncle Vanya with the brutish self-assurance of Stanley Kowalski. Within the range of acceptable interpretations, some may prove to concretize the text in way that brings out a greater depth and complexity in the main text, a greater richness of manifestative qualities. So it is that lines, often heard before in earlier productions as unnecessary or trivial, become alive and memorable, and the relationships between lines take on a clarity never experienced before. No production can be definitive; not all manifestative qualities can necessarily be concretized with equal strength in a given production; the very strength of a certain choice on Line A may push Line B into the shadows. As Ingarden notes, "the literary work is never *fully* grasped in *all* of its strata and components, but only partially" (1973 *Literary Work*, 334). This is as true for productions as for solitary readings.

The techniques that playwrights use to suggest certain emotional states and narrow the range of possible interpretations will be investigated at length in later chapters. Some immediate words of caution, however, are necessary here: tracking down manifestative qualities is an arduous pastime. Even in performance, these qualities are intimated rather than directly presented, and, in the text itself, these qualities are even weaker, being only the intimation of an intimation. Moreover, since manifestative qualities lack precise lexical definition, the same action may indicate different emotions in different contexts. A raised voice does not always indicate anger, and a smile may mask intense disgust. Silence is the most difficult action to analyze, since it communicates nothing in itself. Whole works, such as Pinter's *A Slight Ache*, have been structured around the ambiguity of a sustained silence. Only an investigation of the entire play can lead to an understanding of those silences. The explanation of individual actions depends on an understanding of the entire character and all of his actions within the context established by the entire text. Critic, actor, and director must move in the hermeneutic circle, searching for the significance of the detail in the whole and constructing a sense of the whole from a multiplicity of details. The text of the play implies its subtext, and critic, actor, and director must move from the explicit to the implicit, from the statement to the act that engendered it.

This is not to imply that criticism is a field for amateur psychoanalysts, vainly searching for the hidden traumas that lurk behind Tamburlaine's overachieving or Timon's antisocial behavior. By "character," I mean the Aristotelian concept of *ethos*, as developed in *Nichomachean Ethics*. For Aristotle, *ethos* is a quality that cannot be directly presented; it is only known and exhibited through human actions:

> as bodies are thought to be movements of the character, and as bodies are discriminated by their movement, so too are characters. (1925, IX:1128:9-13)

And:

> a state of character is determined by its activities and its objects. (1925, IX:1122b:1-2)

Just as a person in everyday life can only be known to others through his actions, so too a dramatic figure can only be known through his actions. In narrative, on the other hand, the narrator can directly inform the reader about the moral and psychological traits of the characters without describing specific actions:

> Oh! But he was a tight-fisted hand at the grindstone, Scrooge! A squeezing, wrenching, grasping, scraping, clutching, covetous, old sinner! Hard and sharp as flint, from which no steel had ever struck out a generous fire; secret, and self-contained, and solitary as an oyster. (Dickens 1978, 76)

Of course, the characters in a play are literary constructs. In life, each action is the result of a complex of motivations, some of which are unknown even to the agent of the action. In literature, we witness the action and infer the motivation, but the motivation is only the illusory cause of the action within the presented world of the text. In life, our speeches are founded in our psychic states, which continue, whether we speak or not. In drama, the psychic states of the characters are illusions created by the playwright, which are founded in the words of the text:

the situation is not an objective reality external to the language; it is an immaterial meaning generated by the language itself. (Veltruský 1976 "Basic Features," 130)

Therefore, the actions and mental processes of the characters need not be bound by the dicta of psychologists. Although literary figures may function in accord with our expectations of behavior gleaned from non-literary experience, they may also frustrate those expectations. Surely the Smiths and Martins of *The Bald Soprano*, the sensationally vacillating protagonists of Beaumont and Fletcher, and the exotically metamorphosing characters of Witkiewicz, for all of their differences, create similar effects of disturbance and delight as they defeat the spectator's expectations of consistent or realistic behavior. In short, a dramatic character is the sequence of actions and the subtextual objectives and motivations implied by those actions, all ascribed to a single figure by the side text. A character may or may not exhibit consistent characteristics.

Speech in the main text, then, has the following qualities: (1) it consists of the linguistic acts performed by characters within the presented world of the play; (2) it reaches beyond that presented world to present *itself* to the spectator; (3) it relies on the spectator's acts of pairing to establish a relationship between the speeches and the psychic states of the characters; (4) it relies heavily on manifestative qualities to indicate the unfolding of psychic states within the characters; (5) it tends to be driven by a desire that hopes to find its end in affecting its interlocutor(s); and (6) it finds its fullest expression in performance rather than reading.

Main Text and Dialogue

The reader may have noticed that the word "dialogue" has not yet appeared, while I have employed less common and more awkward terms, such as "dramatic speech," "main text," "utterance," etc. "Dialogue" at last makes its appearance, and it will quickly become obvious that the term is fraught with peril for the dramatic critic. According to the *Oxford English Dictionary*, it has been a common term designating the main text since the eighteenth century, and *that* meaning has, in turn, been so colored by the primary meaning of "dialogue," conversation between two people, that the truly "dramatic" main text has been considered by some to be a dialogue (Szondi 1959, 16). Theatrically effective monologues immediately come to mind and question that assumption; Beckett's *Krapp's Last Tape*, Pinter's *Monologue*, Cocteau's *The Human Voice*, along with the best of the recent spate of one-performer shows too numerous to mention. Besides these cases, which might be dismissed as exotic exceptions to the rule, there are the many long speeches that have been a part of drama since at least the days of Aeschylus. If long speeches are not inherently dramatic, why are they found in the plays of O'Neill and Marlowe, Calderon and Schiller, Plautus and Shakespeare? All four plays under investigation here contain extended passages that cannot be considered dialogic in any usual sense.

The term "dialogue," along with its adjectival term, "dialogic" has recently been used along quite specific lines, defined by the work of Russian formalist Mikhail Bakhtin. At first, it might seem that drama would be the ideal area for Bakhtinian exploration, with its emphasis on dialogic interaction and the carnivalesque, but as Wise (1989, 15-21), has demonstrated, Bakhtin appropriates many of the elements of theatre in order to develop an aesthetics of the fiction that gives first place to the novel. The centrality of the novel in Bakhtin's generic system does indeed make it a valuable tool for those "comparatists and other theoreticians intent on fetishizing prose" (Wise, 15), but renders its applicability to drama problematic. With the exception of one useful phrase that I will borrow from Bakhtin in my chapter on John Osborne, I will leave the questions of Bakhtin's usefulness for another study.

More important, however, is the fact that the aspects of dramatic speech defined in the first part of this chapter do not mention character interaction. The main text often takes the form of a dialogue, but the main text need not be a dialogue. Indeed, not all dialogues are intrinsically dramatic. They may manifest virtually no psychic states and not require production to be fully appreciated.

Since most drama does include two or more interacting speakers, however, it is evident that those verbal exchanges we call "dialogue" play an important role in the projection of psychic states. In order to have a vocabulary sufficiently precise to deal with this interaction, I will reserve the term *main text* to denote the speeches spoken by characters within the presented world of the play, and "dialogue" to designate the illusion of conscious verbal interaction between two or more characters. The alternatives to dialogue are soliloquy, aside, and direct address to the audience. *Dialogue* is obviously a very general term, and not all forms of dialogue as presented in the works of Mukařovský, Veltruský, and Gadamer will furnish us with a more precise critical vocabulary, and allow us to consider various types of verbal intercourse and their dramatic potential.

In "Two Studies of Dialogue" Jan Mukařovský (1977, 84-94) isolates three constant aspects of dialogue, as it appears both in life and in literature: (1) an alternation between speaker and interlocutor; (2) the situating of the speakers in a specific space and time; and (3) semantic reversals. All three aspects are present in all dialogue to some extent, but one of them will tend to dominate at any given instant. When the alternation between speaker and interlocutor dominates, the conflict between "You" and "I" appears most strongly, and result is a *dispute*. In a dispute the relationship between the speakers and the expressive characteristics resulting from the dynamics of that relationship dominate the other aspects. When the relationship of the speakers to their specific spatial and temporal situation dominates, and the speakers direct their attention toward their physical setting, it is a *situational discourse*. The third aspect, the presence of semantic reversals, is by far the most complex of the three. This aspect has three requirements: (1) the speakers must deal with a common subject; (2) the common subject must be evaluated differently by the speakers; and (3) the opposition must be disinterested, as contrasted with the emotional opposition of the dispute. Mukařovský labels this free play of semantic reversals *conversations* and finds this the most purely aesthetic orientation toward dialogue. Lacking the aggressiveness of the dispute, the speakers in a conversation are free to enjoy the eloquence with which they develop the topic and the grace with which they formulate each observation.

Mukařovský errs, however, when he concludes that, since the conversation is the most aesthetic form of dialogue in everyday life, it is also the most satisfying mode of dramatic speech. In a conversation, the participants enjoy each other's eloquence with a detachment that would be threatened or destroyed by the aggressive stance that a dispute demands. The theatrical spectator, on the other hand, is separated from the imaginary world in which the dispute is taking place and can enjoy the style and cunning with which the characters wound and expose each other, even when the participants are far from enjoying it themselves. Because the spectator's privileged status as observer is not threatened by the mode of dialogue used onstage, it is possible for any of Mukařovský's modes to be aesthetically perceived by the spectator.

Mukařovský's identification of dramatic speech and conversation is, moreover, threatened by the fact that a main text can be extremely eloquent and still fail to be theatrically effective. There is no necessary correlation between rhetorical sophistication and effective dramatic speech. The great classical dramatists were able to fuse rhetorical eloquence with the manifestation of psychic states, yet such a fusion is neither necessary nor universally desirable. Eloquence can easily cease being active speech and become fustian or static conversation, as in the Senecan tragedies of the Renaissance, or the euphuistic comedies of John Lyly:

> GERON: What fortune hath thrust you to this distress?
> EUMENIDES: I am going to Thessaly, to seek remedy for Endymion, by dearest friend, who hath been cast into a dead sleep almost these twenty years, waxing old and ready for the grave, being almost but newly come forth of the cradle.
> GERON: You need not for recure travel far, for whoso can clearly see the bottom of this fountain shall have remedy for anything.
> EUMENIDES: That, methinketh, is unpossible. Why, what virtue can there be in water? (Lyly, *Endymion* III. iv. 23-36)

This exchange is decorous and elegant, yet it seems strangely wooden and undramatic. The speeches are public proclamations that seem to lack the intimacy or casualness demanded by the dramatic situation. The formal style makes it sound as if the expressions were fashioned long before they were ever said. The speeches do not "play," i.e., they do not reveal manifestative qualities. How much more theatrical, though less eloquent, is this exchange from Bond's *Saved*:

LEN: Did yer take yer medicine? (*Pause.*) Feelin' better?
PAM: I'm movin down t' me own room t'morra. Yer'll 'ave
  t' move back up 'ere.
LEN: Quieter up 'ere.
PAM: Like a blinking' grave.
LEN: Why don't yer 'ave the telly up?
PAM: No.
LEN: Easy fix a plug.
PAM: Did yer see Fred?
LEN: Yer never took yer medicine (1965, 34-35).

This passage is theatrically effective, yet differs greatly from Mukařovský's ideal of stage dialogue. Not only are the characters uninterested in speaking eloquently, but they are totally lacking in eloquence as well. They are immersed in their personal problems. Len is trying to establish a close and emotionally satisfying relationship with Pam, who cannot understand him and is attracted to Fred. They do not share a common topic of conversation in the passage. Although the dialogue ostensibly deals with the room, Fred, and Pam's medicine, the relationship between the characters serves as the primary source of unity, rather than any opposing statements about a common topic. Semantic reversals are not the soul of drama. Actors cannot play mere linguistic patterns; linguistic patterns are complete in themselves and do not require performance. It is language in the process of revealing psychic states as they manifest themselves in action, language as it indicates the evanescent presence of what can never be directly perceived, what requires performance. This paramount function of dramatic speech is to be found in Mukařovský's triad (if it is to be found there at all) in the dispute, the single aspect that is anchored in the relationship of speaker and interlocutor. The dispute has always been a particularly valuable device, since the conflict between the speakers can heighten their emotional states, break down any veneer of polite behavior, and allow psychic states of rage, frustration, and resentment to surface through the main text. Many of the most memorable couples in dramatic literature are remembered for their disputes; Jason and Medea, Petruchio and Kate, Laura and the Captain, George and Martha, would not be remembered had they not sparred. So, Freytag and Archer were correct when they noted that conflict is a major ingredient in drama, although they failed to explain why this is so. Dramatic conflict is not the end of drama in itself, but a means of structuring a compelling presentation of psychic states. The dispute helps develop tensions and provoke responses that make the speeches active discourse, but the dispute is not the only way of developing a highly emotional scene.

Mukařovský's essay is valuable for differentiating between three kinds of dialogue, though he does not apply them to drama correctly. He fails to realize that any study of dramatic literature must move beyond the linguistic structures, and the semantic reversals contained within them, to a consideration of the relationship of the main text to the prelinguistic states of the characters and the entire extralinguistic situation that unfolds along with the main text.

Jiri Veltruský seems to have recognized some of the shortcomings of his colleague's approach. His essays, "Basic Features of Dramatic Dialogue" (1976) and "The Construction of Semantic Contexts," (1976) cite Mukařovský's work on dialogue, and can be considered elaborations of certain concepts latent in those earlier. Veltruský expands on the second aspect, specific situation in time and space, concentrating on the category least developed by Mukařovský. The situation is no longer merely physical, but embraces the psychological situation in which the characters find themselves as well. Each speech finds its motivation in the extralinguistic situation and is a response to it. At the same time, each speech modifies the context from which it emerges. There is a continual dialectic between the extralinguistic situation and speech. As a result of this dialectic, the dialogue is unified on both the linguistic and the extralinguistic levels. On the linguistic level, the dialogue is unified by repeated words and phrases, the presence of conjunctions and relative pronouns, and by rhetorical devices such as antithesis and parallelism. On the extralinguistic level, it is unified by the spatial, temporal, and psychological situation in which it occurs. The unification of the dialogue emerges through the linguistic devices, revealing the interaction of the speakers within the situation. Consider, for example, the interaction between linguistic and extralinguistic links in this interchange from Harold Pinter's *The Lover*:

> RICHARD: Lover come? (*She does not reply.*) Sarah?
> SARAH: What? Sorry. I was thinking of something
> RICHARD: Did your lover come?

SARAH: Oh yes. He came.
RICHARD: In good shape?
SARAH: I have a headache actually.
RICHARD: Wasn't he in good shape?
(*Pause.*)
SARAH: We all have our bad days. (Pinter 1967, 30)

Richard's obsession with his wife's paramour is manifested by the fact that the lover is the subject of each of Richard's sentences, even though Sarah only makes one explicit reference to him. Richard's insistent questioning forms the impetus for the exchange. Sarah's apparent disinterest in the subject is manifested by her inability to respond directly to her spouse's questions. She does not reply to his first question, then explains that she did not hear it. After finally answering his first question briefly, she does not answer the following question correctly, misunderstanding the intended subject of the sentence. Richard restates the question, adding the subject of the sentence this time. Her answer does not directly refer to his question; she does not make the lover the subject of her sentence. Rather, the linguistic link is provided by the contrast of her predicate "our bad days," with the predicate in his question, "in good shape." Richard's insistent queries, expressed through repeated verbal links, reveal his interest in the lover, while Sarah's evasion of those links reveal her unwillingness to discuss the subject with her husband. Richard's semantic context is dominated by the lover, while Sarah's context only unwillingly admits him.

In the passage from *Saved*, quoted above (19-20), there are even fewer links on the linguistic level. Len answers his own question about Pam's medicine, though the linguistic link is weakened by the intervening lines. Len comments that the room is quieter than the rest of the apartment, and Pam responds by complaining about the quietness, without carrying over a single word from his assertion into her response. Len makes two statements about the possibility of bringing a television set into the room, but the link between the two statements is implicit; the "plug" of the second assertion is synecdochically related to the "telly" of the first. The primary links in the exchange are extralinguistic. Len and Pam are situated in the room at a certain point in their relationship. Len remains positive, concerned, and conciliatory. Pam remains negative and remote. The distance between the two characters is expressed through the lack of linguistic links. Veltruský observes that, if the linguistic level dominates, one tends to have an explanation or clarification of the situation, but if the extralinguistic situation dominates, the sequence tends to stress the chain of actions and reactions among the characters (Veltruský 1976 "Basic Features," 129). The linguistic links dominate in the passage from Lyly's *Endymion*, while the extralinguistic links tend to dominate in the passage from *Saved*. The two passages contain both linguistic and extralinguistic links, however, since the spectator would have no sense of extralinguistic interaction while reading the text if there were absolutely no linguistic links; "unification proceeds on both planes because it cannot be achieved on either one alone" ("Basic Features," 129). The contrast between the linguistic and extralinguistic links is useful, since it connects the main text with the characters, instead of merely defining dramatic speech as the free play of semantic contexts.

Veltruský's theory, however, is limited by its identification of dramatic speech with dialogue. ("Basic Features," 129-130). Veltruský never mentions the problem posed to this theory by monologue or soliloquy in these essays, and it is not clear whether he would consider them inherently non-dramatic devices or not. There is no reason why this theory should limit itself to dialogue, since a monologue is equally able to interact dialectically with its extralinguistic situation. Indeed, a monologue must refer to its extralinguistic context if it is to manifest psychic states and actions. The word "dialogue," by its very derivation and meaning, requires an alternation of speakers. Yet it is not valid to transfer that definition to all kinds of dramatic speech only because most main texts have been written in dialogic form. It is possible that Veltruský mistook the identification of dialogue with the dramatic because of the predominance of realistic conventions in European drama of the late nineteenth and early twentieth centuries. Ibsen and his followers tended to avoid the soliloquy in their realistic dramas, which are constructed as a series of dialogues. Veltruský is not the only critic who was strongly influenced by the realistic movement in his definition of dramatic kind. Una Ellis-Fermor (1964, 242) presents realist drama as the epitome of dramatic kind, though not without acknowledging the inherent limitation of such purity. Judging from his statements and choice of examples (Shaw, Wilde, Moliere, and O'Neill), Veltruský's dramatic model is similar to Ellis-Fermor's. Such a model is inadequate for the analysis of many contemporary dramas.

Using *An Enemy of the People* as a touchstone of purity, the six plays under consideration here are all obviously impure. The selection of realistic drama as a touchstone is more the result of expectations engendered by the dominant style of a period rather than any inherent aspect of dramatic form. As a result of this selection, Veltruský talks about the importance of the extralinguistic situation but spends most of his time analyzing the play of linguistic contexts with little reference to that extralinguistic situation. Theoretically, his essays present an advance on Mukařovský's, but he seems hesitant to pursue his observations to their conclusions in the analysis of dramatic passages.

Unlike Veltruský and Mukařovský, Hans-Georg Gadamer does not intend his theory of dialogue to be synonymous with his view of the theatre; indeed, the two differ substantially. His definition of dialogue, far removed from any definition of dramatic speech, reveals another possible meaning of the term. Gadamer's definition establishes a model of the relationship between the reader and the text, heavily influenced by the Platonic notion of dialectic. In this model, the participants are motivated by a common desire to discover the truth (Gadamer 1976, 66-67). The utterances of the speaker are matched by the attempt of the interlocutor to completely receive the meaning of what is said, and the resultant flow of language is determined by the dialectical development of the thought. The participants share a single train of thought, just as adept participants in a game forget their personal relationships and concentrate on the process of the game, playing it as well as they can.

Gadamer's concept of *dialectical conversation* is inherently undramatic. To the extent that the desire for truth is shared by both speakers, disputation and conflict are minimized, manifestative qualities become relatively unimportant, and the topic under discussion dominates the expressions. Thus, as we noted earlier, the Platonic dialogue, despite its dialogic form, has little dramatic quality. In contrast to philosophic discourse, however, dramatic dialogue generally subordinates the pure desire for knowledge to other desires, desires that require the agency of other characters to achieve their ends. Roman Ingarden has referred to this language, which seeks to effect the behavior of its hearer, as *active discourse* (1973 *Literary Work*, 388), and has rightly noted that this is the dominant form of discourse in drama.

Although they differ in many respects, both Mukařovský's idea of conversation and Gadamer's dialectic conversation differ from active discourse insofar as they minimize the importance of manifestative qualities and the extralinguistic context. In Gadamer, they are subordinated to a search for truth, and in Mukařovský, they are subordinated to the aesthetic qualities of disinterested discourse. Both of these concepts lack reference to an extralinguistic situation. They are self-contained, not requiring any reference on the part of the spectator to the psychic acts of their participants . Furthermore, neither the conversation nor the dialectical conversation require the presence of a spectator for their completion; the affective qualities of both pertain entirely to the participants, and not to any postulated spectator.

Active dramatic dialogue shares qualities of the conversation and the dispute. Without an extralinguistic context shared by the speakers, whether by opposition or a common topic, dialogic interaction quickly exhausts itself and the main text lapses into monologues or silence.

Gadamer's conception of dialectical conversation has other implications for the study of dramatic speech. Every statement, Gadamer (1976, 67) explains, is situated within the totality of discourse. In other words, although a statement may answer one question, it simultaneously calls forth an infinite number of further questions and an infinite number of potential responses. Therefore, there is no absolute beginning or end to a dialectical conversation (1976, 67). Every expression, insofar as it makes a claim to truth, establishes its linguistic context as a monologic assertion; the terms it establishes and the meaning given to those terms by the speaker demand the acceptance of the interlocutor. But, even while it is establishing its claim to truth, it is eliciting questions, qualifications and denials. Each expression is an action, an attempt to alter the situation, to assert itself. And while it asserts itself in its very formation, it also invites its examination. In a play, the examination can come directly from another character within the presented world:

JONSON: D'ye like the quiet?
SHAKESPEARE: What quiet? (Bond 1973, 30-31)

Or the statement can be questioned by the speaker himself. In *Inadmissible Evidence*, Bill Maitland revises or rejects his earlier statements without any pressure or challenge from other characters. Or the dramatist may lead the spectator to question a speech which is unquestioned by either the speaker or his interlocutors, though the establishment of parallels, emotional qualities, or by the effect the speech has on the action of the play. No character in *Bingo* examines the Puritan zeal and self-righteousness of the Son, yet his cold-hearted treatment of his retarded father and his similarities to the most unsympathetic figure in the play, Judith, render all of his statements problematic.

Although any expression may theoretically open the doorway to unlimited discourse, a literary text is finite. A playwright who attempts to include all the potential responses to a statement is not only doomed to total frustration, but he will also sacrifice aesthetic coherence. The playwright must arrange the material so the spectator is not more fascinated by what has been omitted from the presented world than what has been included. Causal links, unity of time and place, unified tone, a protagonist, a thesis, a motif cluster, are but a few of the devices use by playwrights to insure a certain cohesiveness in their work. The degree of compactness and selectivity will vary according to the genre and the subject matter; Yeats' *Calvary* is obviously more selective than the York Corpus Christi play, yet even the most sweeping epic is highly selective. In drama, the objectives of the characters radically limit the potential action. The dramatist defines the scope of potential directions and varieties of actions by assigning the characters limited objectives. Since they are not oriented toward the unlimited investigation of truth, their objectives can be fulfilled or frustrated within the few hours of the play's action. Eliza Dolittle is not interested in truth; she wants to be a lady in a flower shop. Henry Higgins is not interested in philosophy; he is too busy trying to prove the validity of his theories. The dialogue develops in the sphere of those interacting objectives and interests. Although the spectator's reflections on the work may continue to develop long after the play is over, discovering deeper meaning within the play, the play itself must be self-sufficient. For a play is not merely a series of intersecting linguistic contexts, it is also the single, unified, monologic utterance of its author. The individual speeches present a multiplicity of contexts, but the play is a unified context in itself, which serves as the ordering principle for all the speeches that comprise it.

Besides the objectives of characters and the plot that results from their interaction, the text can be unified through the use of motives and themes. By motifs, I mean, "such textual elements as actions, statements revealing states of mind, or feelings, gestures, or meaningful environmental settings" (Falk 1967, 2) and themes, the abstractions that emerge from those motifs. Themes cut across the objectives and speeches of individual characters, and create correspondences and contrasts, unifying actions that are not linked either through the actions of a single character, or through causal links. In certain playwrights and genres, thematic coherence is relatively slight, and the work is unified almost entirely through plot, as in the murder mysteries of Agatha Christie and the farces of Ben Travers. In other works, thematic coherence may be the primary mode of unifying the work, as in Strindberg's Chamber Plays and the dramatic works of the Surrealists. Besides lending coherence, motifs can enrich the expressive quality of a work, as the emotive force of individual events are linked to larger patterns of thought and feeling.

In conclusion, we can state that dramatic dialogue, though not the only form of dramatic discourse, has special qualities that render it most useful to the playwright. It allows manifestative qualities to merge through its disputatious qualities, which are established through clashing linguistic contexts. These linguistic contexts effect, and are effected by, the extralinguistic context which they found. Characters interact and alter their situations as they engage in active discourse, using language to move their hearers toward a particular end. Although all discourse is potentially infinite, dramatic dialogue assumes certain limitations, defined by the finite objectives and interests of its speakers, thereby limiting the potential range of actions, and helping to insure the aesthetic unity of the drama.

RUNNING OUT OF WORDS: "INADMISSIBLE EVIDENCE"

Ever since the epoch-making premiere of *Look Back in Anger* established John Osborne in the vanguard of contemporary English drama overnight, critics have largely agreed that his greatest strength lies, not in plot, thesis or characterization, but in the vigor of his language and rhetorical effectiveness of his tirades (Barnham 1969, 2; Brown 1972, 135). His protagonists--Jimmy Porter (*Look Back in Anger*), Martin Luther (*Luther*), Leonado (*A Bond Honored*), Pamela (*Time Present*), and Laurie (*A Hotel in Amsterdam*), all owe whatever theatrical vitality they have to their acerbic and energetic speeches. *Inadmissible Evidence*, Osborne's most sophisticated and rhetorically varied work to date, is structured around the progressive self-revelation of Bill Maitland, a slightly shady middle-aged lawyer facing the breakup of his career, his domestic life, and his love affair. Maitland is onstage throughout the play; every speech and action witnessed by us is present to his consciousness. Although it has been argued that the events of the play expressionistically mirror Maitland's consciousness (Barnham 1969, 68-69), it is perhaps more accurate to say that Maitland provides a focus for the thematic concerns that develop in the course of the play. Maitland's personal and professional dilemmas are less important in themselves than as vehicles conveying certain psychic states; isolation, alienation, self-accusation, guilt, and rage.

The causal sequence of events is relatively unimportant; the exterior conditions of the protagonist's life do not differ substantially from his dilemma as it was presented in the initial trial sequence. Instead of developing a tightly-knit plot, unified by causal relationships, Osborne unfolds the implications of his opening scene through a sequence of monologues, collective monologues, partially overheard telephone conversations, and dialogues.

Inadmissible Evidence does not generate its primary expressive qualities through the clash of a protagonist and an antagonist. Simon Trussler (1969, 120-125) has noted that Osborne is rarely able to create worthy opponents for his heroes. Indeed the heroes are sometimes deeply troubled by their very inability to find a worthy opponent. The major tension in *Inadmissible Evidence*, as in so many of Osborne's plays, is found within the protagonist. Maitland does not develop through his opposition to other characters; he does not need an antagonist to reveal to him the truth about himself. Maitland carries out a dialectical process within himself. Insofar as he questions and corrects the limitations of his own discourse rather than accepting it as true, his speeches do not have the monologic integrity and consistency of semantic context that Mukařovský (1977, 109-110) and Bakhtin (1973, 150-156) would isolate as pure monologue. The following passage illustrates Maitland's restless and repeated emendations of his own assertions:

> However, however, my lord. I seem to retain very little. Very little indeed, hardly anything at all, in fact. Which is disturbing. Because I don't see how I can carry on my work even, well I am carrying on with it, but I must be getting less and less any good at it. *Even* my work, that's almost the least of it, which is probably no doubt why I find myself here, in the dark dock arraigned before you. But both my clients and colleagues seem to think, at least they used to think, I had a sort of dashing flair for making decisions, which might have been true to some extent. This can't hide the fact from me, and never has done, that I am by nature indecisive. (Osborne 1965, 18)

No one challenges anything Maitland says in this speech; he realizes that his previous claims have been inaccurate and attempts to correct them. He replaces "very little" with "hardly anything at all," asserts that his clients "seem to think" that he can make decisions, but quickly transfers "think" into the past tense. The one assertion that begins as a defense ("But both my clients and colleagues seem to think...") collapses into self-accusation ("I am by nature indecisive"). The attempt at self-defense is defeated by self-awareness, rather than any outside force. We are made aware of a fragmented and critical consciousness that cannot accept its own assertions. In his study of Dostoevsky, Bakhtin (1973, 186) observed a similar shifting of linguistic contexts within the speeches of a single character and labeled this device, "dialogization of monologue." Lacking both the unified linguistic context that distinguishes monologue, and the alternation of speaker and interlocutor that distinguishes dialogue, the dialogized monologue manifests psychic fragmentation and intense self-awareness. The speaker makes a prelinguistic judgment, articulates it, and, upon listening to that utterance, finds it inadequate, and in need of amendment or even repudiation. Of course, the process of judgment, expression, listening, and evaluation can be extremely rapid, but the dialogized monologue exhibits a highly sophisticated sequence of discrete acts. In *Inadmissible Evidence*, the dialogized monologue is Maitland's characteristic mode of discourse. He is sufficiently intelligent to perceive the weakness of his own rationalizations and defenses, and uncertain enough to alternately defend and doubt his own assertions.

Inadmissible Evidence can be interpreted as a single extended utterance, dominated by the protagonist, from his hesitant and incoherent opening statement, to his final silence as he waits alone in his office. The play begins with a striking and disorienting scene, as Maitland dreams himself on trial on some sort of morals charge. Pleading "not guilty," he takes the stand in his own defense, but his speech, rather than the polished periods of an attorney, are rambling, disjointed, and verge on nonsense. This is our initiation to this presented world; a distorted and somewhat fantastic presentation of a trial, in which the fundamental motifs and themes of the play are introduced:

> In the facts, above all the facts, inescapable. Anna, my wife, Hudson, I mean my managing clerk, Hudson, Joy, the telephonist, the enrichment of our standard of living, I've lost my prescription, Jane, my father's too old to be here, thank God, the National Research, Research Development

Council, the Taylor Report, the Nayler Report, failure
report, and a projected budget of five hundred thousand
million, millions for this purpose, the practical dangers of
premarital in the commanding heights of our declining
objects. (11)

In this torrent of verbal fragments, the lack of syntactical subordination, causal links and pauses helps to convey the sense of confusion and anxiety that underlies many of Maitland's actions. Government expenditures, medicine, domestic and professional relationships exist in alogical juxtaposition. The only explicit linguistic link is the nonsensical rhyme progression, Taylor-Nayler, failure. Syntactical relationships are often unclear; "Hudson" appears to be in apposition to "my wife," until Maitland explains that Hudson is actually his managing clerk, and that "my wife" belongs to "Anna" as an appositive. The budget's apparent purpose, "the practical dangers of pre-marital in the commanding heights of our declining objects," is neither grammatically well-formed (since the adjective "pre-marital" lacks a noun) nor is it a coherent statement. It reveals Maitland's feelings of personal, professional, and social failure, but this fragmented utterance cannot be understood as a description of an objectively existing state of affairs in the presented world of the play. It is unified by the subjective state of the speaker, not an objective state of affairs. The absence of linguistic links draws attention to the extralinguistic context and the emotional state of the speaker, rather than clarifying the objective relationships that exist within the presented world.

 The absence of syntactical links, as well as logical, casual, and sequential patterns of organization, allows Osborne to compress all the major themes and motifs of his play into the opening speeches. Four of the major characters are first mentioned in the passage quoted above, but we must wait for further information before the importance of those references can be appreciated. The reference to the prescription, to take another example, is the first of many references to Maitland's migraines and the medicine he takes for them.

 Some of the secondary motifs are set up here only to be developed much later in the play. The reference to the father, for example, only takes on substantial thematic significance near the end of the second act. A short time before the play began, Maitland tells his daughter Jane, he went to visit his father, who refused to recognize him. Osborne saves this information for the scene in which his protagonist tries to make contact with his own daughter, thus providing a very minor, unseen character as a motivic counterpoint to the confrontation of the protagonist with the only member of his family who appears onstage.

Because the initial trial scene does not have any causal effect on the ensuing action, Carter (1969, 88) has called it an excrescence, and has suggested it belongs more properly at the end of the second act than at the beginning of the first. Carter does not appreciate how the scene serves several important functions in its present position. First, it establishes that non-realistic conventions function as a means of presentation within the world of the play. Without this introduction, Maitland's later non-realistic scenes, such as his appointment with Mrs. Tonks, would appear stylistically at odds with the earlier, realistic scenes. The opening scene establishes from the start that the presented world of *Inadmissible Evidence* is one that is not bound by realistic stage conventions. Secondly, the scene establishes the image of Maitland's trial as the play's dominant theatrical and structural metaphor. The legal procedures, official documents, and questions of guilt and innocence that pervade the realistic sections of the play become charged with metaphorical significance in the context established by this initial scene. Maitland's attempt to defend himself, at first incoherent, turns more into a confession as it grows more focused: judgment becomes self-judgment. The dominant image, the lawyer on trial, comes to inform all subsequent legal actions in the play.

It also contributes to establishing Maitland's absolute centrality. Because *he* is on trial here, all the motifs connected with him are given greater import. His migraine headaches, drinking, philandering, and professional misconduct in themselves may lack the magnitude required of a dramatic protagonist, especially one who dominates a play to the extent that Bill Maitland does. Each problem in itself may be considered petty, and an accumulation of petty problems does not in itself confer stature. Osborne introduces the problems in an enigmatic and tantalizing manner, mixing personal confessions with allusions to contemporary Britain, and unifying them all through the speaker's paradoxical position, as he defends himself in court while admitting all his shortcomings. This role takes on a further urgency as we realize that this is a dream in which he has put himself on trial, making him play at once the roles of defendent, judge, and prosecution. This self-division and its attendant anguish invests all of Maitland's actions with greater intensity and magnitude. As a dramatic character, Bill Maitland comes to demand our attention by virtue of his emotions rather than his actions. It is what he suffers, not what he does, that makes him compelling. His deeds would fail to interest us if his underlying complexities were not made apparent.

The first scene establishes the interior qualities that invest and inform the rest of the protagonist's actions. For example, when Maitland tells Hudson about his work with Bennet, a youth charged with indecent assault:

> We didn't get very far. He was too upset. Clothes off, possessions signed for, bath, medical inspection in the whistling cold, keys jangling. He wasn't in any state for anything. I don't know why we do any criminal work. (36)

The vividness of this brief description, including temperature, sound, and the emotional state of the client, followed by Maitland's final, slightly despairing, comment, help to manifest his sympathy for Bennet's situation. The speech takes on added power, however, because it manifests echoes of Maitland's dream narration of his own prison experience in the opening scene:

> I have always been quite certain that this is where I would end up, here, I've seen it too many times, with you there and counsel over there. There. And there. Down to the cells. Off to the scrubs, hands over your watch and your money, take all your clothes off, have a bath, get examined, take all your clothes off in the cold, and the door shut behind you. (19)

On a level of psychological realism, it could be said that the experience with Bennett at the Scrubs provided the impetus for the dream, and that Maitland's later conversation with Hudson reveals the genesis of certain elements in the dream itself. More importantly, however, on the level of dramatic construction, Maitland's degree of identification with Bennett (who, like Maitland in his dream, has been accused of an indecent act) is established circuitously. His speech to Hudson is much more heavily charged with personal identification and empathy than the speech itself, unattached from the opening scene, would indicate. It is only because we have seen Maitland's dream that we understand how thoroughly two very different roles, that of lawyer and accused sexual offender, are being brought together by the imagination of the protagonist. The professional activities of the law office become the external and realistic variations of the trial theme, which finds an internal and poetic treatment in the opening scene. These activities provide distinct and concrete vehicles for the manifestation of Maitland's anxiety, and his emotions, in turn, charge the language of his professional routine with richer manifestative qualities. Carter's criticism of the first scene ignores the emotional richness that the scene lends to the realistic depiction of professional routine and office gossip that immediately follow it.

But if the manifestative qualities did not develop beyond the emotional range established by the first scene, *Inadmissible Evidence* would soon be unbearable, since it relies almost exclusively on the dynamic presentation of the protagonist's psychic states to animate it. There are no theses or provocative issues to consider, the plot is negligible, and suspense virtually non-existent. Osborne has stated that he believes his purpose as a dramatist is to make audiences feel more deeply, and his best work is not distinguished by greater intellectual sophistication, but by more complex and varied expressive qualities (Hayman 1972, 140). Given Osborne's aesthetic aim and his consequent subordination of all his materials and techniques to that aim, it is necessary that the subsequent scenes in *Inadmissible Evidence* continue to exhibit variety in the types and intensity of emotions manifested.

In life, a person may repeatedly express a certain emotion, and the repeated expression in no way exhausts the psychic state that provides the grounding for that expression. In the theatre, on the other hand, the main text does not merely serve to express the psychic state of the speakers, but also expresses it in an aesthetic form that is presented to us. Each time that a character repeats the same expression of the same psychic state, the strength of the statement is dissipated somewhat. Each repetition of the same aspect of a psychic state detracts from the maximum potential of the state's expressive power. (This is not to say that each repetition of an expression is an aesthetic flaw, The same combination of words may come to express a variety of psychic states, due to shifting contexts, so that the total import of the expression varies with each utterance. It is only when a passage reiterates the same meaning to us without contextual change or nuance that the utterance is flawed.)

Director Peter Brook explains:

> There is a joy in violent shocks; the only trouble with violent shocks is that they wear off. What follows a shock? Here's the snag. I fire a pistol at a spectator--I did so once--and for a second I have a possibility to reach him in a different way. I must relate this possibility to a purpose, otherwise a moment later he is back where he was:inertia is the greatest force we know. I show a sheet of blue--nothing but the colour blue--blueness is a direct statement that arouses an emotion, the next second that impression fades: I hold up a brilliant flash of scarlet--a different impression is made, but unless someone can grab this moment, knowing why and how and what for--it too begins to wane. (1969, 54-55)

Every theatrical artist must deal with the problem Brook formulates here. Every theatrical sign begins to diminish in power immediately after its appearance. Similarly, any extended manifestation of a single aspect of a psychic state quickly begins to lose its theatrical effectiveness. Since an emotional state has no intellectual content or complexity of its own, it must develop through verbal contrast and transformation. Every psychic state has a potential for expression. As it realizes that potential, it exhausts it. In other words, any emotion expressed onstage becomes spent, progressively disqualifying itself for further dramatic development even as it reaches its fullest expression. Aesthetically, Maitland's fear expresses itself and exhausts its potential for further effectiveness simultaneously.

In *Inadmissible Evidence*, Maitland's process of personal exhaustion is expressed through the simultaneous expression and exhaustion of emotional states presented in the play itself. The initial anxiety, fear, bitterness and desperation are presented, and replaced, as the possibility of reiterating them is theatrically exhausted, by the tenderness and resignation of the final scenes. Just as Maitland's passion is spent, so is the play's language; the final silence reveals the exhaustion of its protagonist's anxiety and language.

Inadmissible Evidence does not generate its primary expressive qualities through the clash of a protagonist and an antagonist. Simon

Trussler (1969, 120-125) has noted that Osborne is rarely able to create worthy opponents for his heroes. Indeed the heroes are sometimes troubled by their very inability to find a worthy opponent. The major tension in *Inadmissible Evidence*, as in so many of Osborne's plays, is found within the protagonist. Maitland does not develop through his opposition to other characters; he does not need an antagonist to reveal to him the truth about himself. Maitland carries out a dialectical process within himself. Insofar as he questions and corrects the limitations of his own discourse rather than accepting it as true, his speeches do not have the monologic integrity and consistency of semantic context that Mukařovský (1977, 109-110) and Bakhtin (1973, 150-156) would isolate as pure monologue. The following passage illustrates Maitland's restless and repeated emendations of his own assertions:

> However, however, my lord. I seem to retain very little. Very little indeed, hardly anything at all, in fact. Which is disturbing. Because I don't see how I can carry on my work even, well I am carrying on with it, but I must be getting less and less any good at it. *Even* my work, that's almost the least of it, which is probably no doubt why I find myself here, in the dark dock arraigned before you. But both my clients and colleagues seem to think, at least they used to think, I had a sort of dashing flair for making decisions, which might have been true to some extent. This can't hide the fact from me, and never has done, that I am by nature indecisive. (18)

No one challenges anything Maitland says in this speech; he realizes that his previous claims have been inaccurate and attempts to correct them. He replaces "very little" with "hardly anything at all," asserts that his clients "seem to think" that he can make decisions, but quickly transfers "think" into the past tense. The one assertion that begins as a defense ("But both my clients and colleagues seem to think. . .") collapses into self-accusation ("I am by nature indecisive"). The attempt at self-defense is defeated by self-awareness, rather than any outside force. We are made aware of a fragmented and critical consciousness that cannot accept its own assertions. In his study of Dostoevsky, Bakhtin (1973, 186) observed a similar shifting of linguistic contexts within the speeches of a single character and labeled this device, "dialogization of monologue." Lacking both the unified linguistic context that distinguishes monologue, and the alternation of speaker and interlocutor that distinguishes dialogue, the dialogized monologue manifests psychic fragmentation and intense self-awareness. The speaker makes a prelinguistic judgment, articulates it, and, upon listening to that utterance, finds it inadequate, and in need of amendment or repudiation.

Of course, the process of judgment, expression, listening, and evaluation can be extremely rapid, but the dialogized monologue exhibits a highly sophisticated sequence of discrete acts. In *Inadmissible Evidence*, the dialogized monologue is Maitland's characteristic mode of discourse. He is sufficiently intelligent to receive the weakness of his own rationalizations and defenses, and uncertain enough to alternately defend and doubt his own assertions.

Maitland's lengthy speeches remain dynamic because they manifest a continual succession of varied psychic states. They never develop a single topic extensively from a single point of view, thus allowing new aspects of Maitland's preoccupations to emerge quickly. His mind is restless, continually modifying or rejecting what he has said earlier. When he is speaking with other characters, he often anticipates their objectives or attitudes before they voice them. He is aware of the criticisms that lie hidden behind Hudson's politic statements and Jones's silences:

> And as for necking, I never went in for it, never would, and pray God I am never so old, servile or fumbling that I ever have to wriggle through that dingy assault course. Do you like it, do you want it, those are the only questions I have ever thought worth while going into. You think I'm not telling the truth? Well, it's as near the truth as I can find at this moment; for one thing I have never had very strong fingers, which is why I had to give up learning the piano. (34)

He begins his speech by asserting his sexual directness and scorn for the niceties of foreplay. The language is emphatic; the triple appearance of "never," along with "only," "ever," and highly colored verbs and adjectives ("servile," "fumbling," "dingy"), manifest an intensity of emotion that verges on the hyperbolic. From this extremity of assertion, he proceeds to verbalize Hudson's unarticulated questioning of his assertion. Suddenly, the assertion of strength and virility is replaced by a humorous and playful admission of weakness. He first admits that his tirade is only as "near the truth" as he is able to make it. He then goes on to lightheartedly admit a lack of physical coordination, which disqualifies him either to be a pianist or a master of foreplay. The aggressive assertion of masculine bravado suddenly gives way to the wry and ironic wit of a fumbling, physically inadequate individual. Maitland's quickness and verbal sophistication mediate between the comic extremes of both positions and effect a humorous juxtaposition of contrasting self-portraits. By performing both positions in close juxtaposition, he exhibits himself as a performer who is superior to either of the positions. Although *Inadmissible Evidence* is constructed around a single character, his mind is sufficiently varied and flexible to provide a variety of contexts. Its ability to anticipate others' reactions reveals a quickness of mind and great mental energy that impels the play forward.

Interestingly, the effectiveness of Osborne's plays seems to exist in direct proportion to the intensity and passionateness of the mental energy expended by their protagonists. Pamela (*Time Present*) and Wyatt (*West of Suez*) are no less eloquent and complex than Jimmy Porter and Bill Maitland, but they lack the energy of those more successful creations, and tend to languish in petulance rather than explode in rage. Petulance is as annoying in literature as in life. Lacking foundation in a passionate state of mind, it does not exhibit sufficient complexity to inform a series of emotional states, or drive the action of a play forward. Because Maitland is an intense character with great emotional range, Shirley's anger, although vehement, does not overshadow him. Since Osborne constructs his plays around a dominant protagonist, the protagonist tends to circumscribe the emotional range of the entire play, and the emotions of all the other characters develop within the orbit of the protagonist. In *Time Present*, all of the characters are subordinated to Pamela, whose emotional range is narrow and whose impulses tend to be superficial. In Osborne, the more limited the protagonist, the more limited the play.

Maitland's energy and protean qualities make him one of Osborne's most successful dramatic figures. His ambivalent attitudes toward both himself and his assertions are mirrored in his unstable relationships with those around him. He alternately manifests an aggressive state of mind, which finds its expression in disputatious speeches and a frightened and dependent frame of mind, in which he attempts conciliation. In his disputatious mode, he stresses the differences between himself and his interlocutors. He often uses this technique in his dialogues with Hudson. Hudson's strategy is to keep the exchange cool and disinterested, on the level of conversation, but Maitland persists in introducing disputatious elements:

> BILL: I know. Anna's my wife. There's never any doubt what side you're on.
> HUDSON: I'm not on any side.
> BILL: Yes you are. Wives and angels. Me: mistressesand devils (40).

Similarly, Maitland stresses the differences between himself and his son, Anna, Jane, Jones, and Liz.

These acts of aggressive differentiation serve two major dramatic functions. First, they establish Maitland's desire for self-definition. He presents verbal self-portraits of himself as isolated from others, yet the very nature of the antithetical relationships he posits between himself and others depends on their presence. If they were absent, he would have no way to define himself. In the example quoted above, Maitland defines himself by saying, in effect, "I am what you [Hudson] are not." It simultaneously manifests aggression and dependence. Secondly, these verbal actions allow Maitland's anger to manifest itself through a dramatic action in which a character becomes the object of his of his general frustration. Instead of lashing out in all directions at once, it is directed toward a particular figure who could react to his aggression and somehow alter the situation. Jones and Hudson refuse to be drawn into a dispute and pretend to ignore his provocations. His beloved daughter remains totally mute. Liz, by contrast, acknowledges them through a gentle response. All the characters are defined in part by the way they respond to the protagonist's invitations to dispute.

Maitland's aggression is generally directed toward characters whom he believes will neither abandon him as a result of this behavior nor retaliate in kind. Yet, when he fears abandonment, he stops his aggression and stresses whatever he might have in common with his interlocutor. When his secretary and ex-lover Shirley announces she is going to quit, he tries to soften her aggressive, disputatious posturing:

SHIRLEY: I just want you to know that I'm giving in my
    notice, that's all. You owe me a week's holiday, but
    I'll give you a week anyway.
BILL: But what for?
SHIRLEY: I've just made up my mind I'm going, that's all.
BILL: Of course I mind--
SHIRLEY: Well, that's bad luck for you, isn't it?
BILL: I don't know, love. Perhaps its bad luck for both of
    us.
SHIRLEY: Not for me it isn't (46).

When Shirley announces her attention to leave, her repeated assertions of disinterest ("just" and "that's all") only serve to manifest her resentment and vindictiveness more strongly, and Maitland is first dismayed and later upset both by her decision and the condemnation of his behavior implicit in it. She constructs an implicit antithesis that manifests her anger--her departure will be "bad luck" for her lecherous employer and "good" for herself. By replacing her antithesis with the suggestion that her decision might be bad for both of them, he attempts to neutralize the anger-charged polarity of her semantic context. But she reasserts her strategy of antithesis, this time presenting herself as the subject of it ("Not for me it isn't"). He finds himself unable to soften her resentful tone, and the scene ends with Shirley delivering an angry speech and rushing from the room before Maitland can answer her. Despite her aggressive veneer, she is unable to assert herself strongly enough to silence her employer's objections, and cuts off the dialogue rather than risk the possibility of defeat in a protracted struggle of wills

Maitland's pacifying tactics in the scene with Shirley are actually similar to those that Hudson and Jones use to ward off the verbal attacks of their employer, Hudson's defensive "I'm not on any side" (40) tries to avoid a dispute by denying the existence of any polarity. There is an important difference, however, between Maitland's use of conciliatory techniques, and Hudson's and Jones's. Their good manners merely cloak their resentment. Jones lacks the honesty to directly challenge his opponent's statements, and retaliates with indirect criticisms:

> JONES: I hear you've lost Mrs. Garnsey.
> BILL: What do you mean *I've* lost Mrs. Garnsey.
> JONES: Well *we've* lost Mrs. Garnsey. The firm has. (76)

Jones accuses Maitland of having bungled the Garnsey case, but immediately retreats at the first possibility of a dispute. Jones and Hudson do not avoid disputes out of a desire to remain close to Maitland, but out of a desire to avoid unpleasantness. Their evasions lack the emotional intensity of Maitland's attempt to salvage his relationship with Shirley. There, Maitland does not refrain from disputing with Shirley out of polite indifference, but because he values whatever genuine qualities their relationship might have had. He avoids disputation because it might lead to estrangement; his colleagues avoid disputation because it might lead to unpleasantness.

Although Maitland's verbal assaults indirectly reveal his dependence on the presence of others, they have the ironic effect of estranging those whom he most fears losing. Aware of the effects his assaults have, he alternates aggression with desperate attempts to maintain contact. The alternation of disputatious and conciliatory statements manifest a strong alternation of emotional impulses within the character. He tries to make Shirley admit that there was some integrity to their relationship; he stresses the differences between himself and Hudson, yet offers him a partnership in the firm; he openly despises Jones yet refrains from firing him; he verbally attacks Liz, Anna, and Jane, yet admits the deep emotional ties he has to each of them.

These violent alternations indicate the emotional frustration that characterizes Osborne's protagonist, and form the basis for the central development in the play. The desire to wound and the desire to maintain a degree of intimacy exist in a tension that is only resolved when Maitland resigns himself to solitude. As I stated earlier, the causal sequence of events in *Inadmissible Evidence* does not essentially modify the state of affairs that was established in the dream trial at the opening of the play. The later action gives fuller expression to that initial state through dramatic incident. As clients, associates and intimates successively withdraw from Maitland, the state of solitude and self-judgment of which Bill had dreamed becomes progressively more real:

> Hello, Liz....I'm frightened....It was as if I only existed because of her, because she allowed me to, but if she turned off the switch....turned off the switch....who knows? (62)

But this desperate anxiety alternates with his desire to be rid of everyone, and to allow the "trial" to commence. He remarks to Anna, "I don't know about Liz. She may be the last to pack it in, but pack it in she will" (64). His solitary self-judgment is both an object of fear and attraction for him. At the end of the play, he gently refuses to return home, deciding that it is better to remain alone in his office "waiting" (115). By the final curtain the fear has been expended and Maitland's vigil for judgment no longer evokes anxiety and desperation. The initial linguistic context established in the opening scene is neither challenged nor undermined by later scenes, but undergoes a process of gradual elaboration and clarification. The manifestative qualities, on the other hand, undergo extensive modification.

In *Inadmissible Evidence*, Maitland's process of personal exhaustion is conveyed through the simultaneous expression and exhaustion of emotional states presented in the play itself. The initial anxiety, fear, bitterness and desperation are presented, and replaced, as the possibility of reiterating them is theatrically exhausted, by the tenderness and resignation of the final scenes. Just as Maitland's passion is spent, so is the play's language; the final silence reveals the exhaustion of its protagonist's anxiety and language. We are brought through a succession of scenes that are constructed to highlight the emotional state of the protagonist, and the play's emotional impact depends on the extent to which we are led to empathize with Maitland, warts and all.

The play began with a torrent of language that followed emotive and associative progressions--the language of dreams. This sense of fragmentation continues throughout the first act, as Maitland's coworkers arrive, and the day's work begins. French scenes are short, and topics shift quickly. Topics become significant, not because they are treated in extended scenes, but because they are briefly brought up a number of times. Maitland's client, Mrs. Garnsey, is mentioned on sixteen different occasions before she enters, although fifteen of these references are very brief. Maitland refers to her between his other activities--talking to his colleagues, coping with his headache, trying to talk to Liz on the telephone, and avoiding work. His extraordinary mental restlessness expresses great energy and demands that we expend equal energy, continually reorienting him/herself as the protagonist's focus shifts. The focus tends to alternate between personal and professional matters, with Maitland trying to avoid work and solve his rapidly disintegrating personal life. The energy that Maitland puts into these various brush fires could easily be comic, even farcical, given the tempo and rhythm that the scenes establish, were the material not so painful. One must turn to the less compassionate imagination of Simon Grey, who turns stories of personal decay into black comedies, using structural devices very like the ones in the first act of *Inadmissible Evidence* in his *Butley* and *Otherwise Engaged*, but with much greater delight in his protagonists' discomfort.

Osborne asks us to be quick and attentive participants, piecing together information that is often fragmentary. The disjointed speeches that open the play are only the most extreme examples of the techniques of disjunctive speech that run through much of the play. While listening to the frequent telephone conversations, for example, we must not only understand what Maitland is saying, but must also attempt to construe the entire dialogue on the basis of Maitland's speeches alone. The interpretative action becomes more complex in the second act, when we are told by the side text that we should even doubt whether there is anyone on the other end (59).

Of course, the most extreme form of disjunction would be a play of verbal nonsense, composed totally of strings of *non sequiturs*, which like Brook's field of blue, would quickly exhaust its potential to communicate meaning. Osborne uses structural techniques to order the disintegrative tendencies of Maitland's language. These techniques include: (1) the constant presence of the protagonist; (2) character consistency; (3) recurring motifs; and (4) a realistic grounding for all plot incidents.

Maitland provides the common focus for the play's many actions. Every character is acquainted with him, and the minor characters are almost exclusively defined by their interaction with his actions and concerns. Mrs. Garnsey, for example, describes how her husband seems to be losing contact with everyone, while Maitland (along with us) see in this description a reflection of his own situation. With Mrs. Tonks, he re-enacts the failure of his own marriage, as Osborne alternates quotations from Mrs. Tonks's depositions with Maitland's own admissions of failure. Even Maples, superficially so different from the protagonist, shares his alternation of nervous energy and exhaustion, his assertiveness and his desire to submit to judgment. If these three scenes were written with a different lawyer advising each client (say, Hudson with Mrs. Garnsey, Jones with Mrs. Tonks, and Maitland with Maples), the explicit connection with the protagonist in each scene would be lost, and the play would become hopelessly diffuse. Maitland provides the point of organization for the many actions and relationships treated in the play; it is through him that they gain coherence.

With the exception of Maitland, the dramatic figures are quite simple, and express a very limited range of emotions and concerns. This limitation is communicated in part by a more limited range of vocabulary and verbal inventiveness. Shirley is wounded and vindictive, Hudson is pleasant and noncommittal. Each of them contributes his/her consistent quality with each entrance.

The milieu offers a degree of continuity, not only because the play's single setting limits the possible actions, but also because the routine and appointments of the law office impose a structure on the chaotic and conflicting impulses that divide Maitland. Without being forced to see his clients, he certainly never would. The sixteen references to Mrs. Garnsey build to her entrance because she is scheduled to come to the office at a certain time, and Maitland cannot avoid seeing her, as much as he wishes he could. The inevitability of the appointment calender replaces the classical concept of Fate and the relentless causality of Scribe and Ibsen. In the second act, just as the appointment with Mrs. Garnsey provided the direction for the first act, the scheduled meeting with Jane provides the climactic incident.

Recurring motifs provide links that cut across intervening material. Each of the references to Mrs. Garnsey momentarily establishes continuity with the growing string of earlier references to her, even though a series of other topics have intervened. Maitland's headaches, drinking, cancerous thumb, professional misconduct, and his problems with offspring, lovers, colleagues, and clients, are all mixed together, and we are made to move from one concern to another, while constantly keeping the other concerns in mind and prepared for further elaboration. Such a structure demands far more of us than the lucid exposition of a well-made play. Just as Maitland is attempting to cope with a jarring array of personal and professional problems, so too we are forced to continually shift our attention as the play develops. Discontinuous repetition of motifs, rather than linear progression, is the stylistic strategy here. Unity is provided by the repetition, while the discontinuity continues to supply a threat of total fragmentation.

Although the entire first act, with the exception of the dream trial, is presented realistically, the second act presents a variety of nonrealistic conventions. The confrontation with Jane, for example, is a tirade to a silent girl, which would be psychologically unconvincing if it were judged according to the realistic conventions that dominated the preceding scene. Yet the presence of each character is justified on the realistic level. Either they have a professional relationship to Maitland, or a personal one. Just as the side text never has the law office disappear, to be replaced by a nonrealistic setting, so too, the motivations for all the French scenes remain within what would be realistically verisimilar in a lawyer's office. Osborne sets limits to his use of nonrealistic conventions.

The second act begins with an extended monologue for Maitland (the two telephone conversations), reverts to a more realistic mode of presentation in three short dialogues of Maitland with Hudson, Joy, and Jones. The mode becomes less realistic again in the Maitland's scenes with his two female clients. The first of these, with Mrs. Tonks, is the most protracted dispute in the play. As she reads from her divorce petition, her lawyer reads extracts from her husband's papers, challenging her assertions. By fragmenting and intercalating the two legal documents, Osborne is able to bring out the clash of linguistic contexts between husband and wife, and allow the actions of plaintiff and defendant to manifest emotions of intense aggression and defensiveness. Not only does this scene present us with a portrait of the Tonks's marriage, but the fact that Maitland is reading the husband's statement and becomes in the steadily mounting tension allows the figures of Mr. Tonks and Maitland to merge. Tonks's marital failure becomes indistinguishable from his wife's lawyer's:

> BILL: To have another child. Another child. In spite of the advice given to her by the Counsel sherefused to use this.
> MRS. T: That it was his desire to have sexual intercourse with a woman in this street to whom he referred....
> BILL: Because she said it was nasty. Nasty and Messy.
> MRS. T: He constantly referred to as "that great big beautiful blonde bat."

BILL: I wonder if it was real or dyed. Not that it matters.
MRS. T: On at least eleven occasions during the marriage he attempted to commit....
BILL: I deny that I persisted.
MRS. T: And did in fact
BILL: There is no truth at all in this. (80)

The sequence is highly presentational. It is not a representation of what might actually occur in a lawyer's office. Nor does it present a purely subjective picture of what Maitland believes is happening. Instead, it theatrically fuses Maitland's personal concerns with his professional activities. His speeches here mix statements of Tonks's with reflections of his own that reveal an inner affinity with Tonks. His parenthetical query about the blonde woman's natural hair color is obviously not in the legal statement, but it furthers the identification of the two men with each other, since it shows that Maitland is not merely functioning as the reader of a text, but is mentally involved in it and is investing it with personal significance. Osborne's use of non-realistic conventions in this scene allows us to see aspects of Maitland that would remain inaccessible in a realistic presentation of Mrs. Tonks's appointment with her lawyer.

The scene also strengthens and elaborates Maitland's personal concern with judgment, this time, through the more specific image of divorce. Divorce becomes a particularly apt image of Maitland's growing isolation. All of the clients we see in *Inadmissible Evidence* are involved in cases where their private lives are made public. The divorce petitions, and Maples' account of his life as a homosexual, are highly personal autobiographical statements, in which no detail is too intimate to escape scrutiny. Law is not seen here as a complex welter of laws and contracts, but rather as the occasion for self-presentation. *Inadmissible Evidence* is no more about the legal system than *King Lear* is about real estate. It simply provides Osborne with a repertoire of images and conventions with which to dramatize his protagonist's plight. Mrs. Tonks exists to help exhibit Maitland's defensiveness in his intimate relationships with women.

The next scene, with Mrs. Andersen, provides a strong contrast with that preceding, acrimonious scene. The fact that the same actress plays both the divorce petitioners lends an added continuity to the scene that went before it, as if the rancor between these two figures has been spent. The tone is pensive and elegiac. There are no disputatious elements here; Maitland's soliloquy is a gentle obbligato to his client's statement. It cannot be called a dialogue; there is no evidence that Mrs. Andersen is aware of her interlocutor's statements. Although her speeches modify the course of Maitland's reveries from time to time, his speeches have no influence on hers. Thus, the scene lacks the dialectical development that characterizes dialogic interaction.

Maitland's comments here are more tranquil. His sentences are longer and switches topics less often. It is a reverie, written in the subjunctive mood, rather than the indicative mood that dominates the rest of the play:

> Perhaps I'd have walked out of that place on my own,
> there's have been no one else, I could have done as I liked.
> I could have sat in Lyons and got myself a cup of coffee and
> a roll and butter all on my own. (86)

This wistful idyll is rendered disturbing by its preoccupation with death and Mrs. Andersen's simultaneous account of her hopeless marriage. Maitland can only find consolation in wistful reflections on what might have been.

The melancholy resignation of the Andersen scene show the play moving toward an emotional resolution for the protagonist, but the play is far from finished. Osborne has established expectations for three characters yet to appear: Maples, Jane, and Liz.

The first of these is both the most unusual the and most subtle. Maples is yet another client, and, as we have seen, Maitland either tends to avoid his clients (like Mrs. Garnsey), or see them as merely objects for his highly personal reveries (Mrs. Tonks and Mrs. Andersen). But, with Maples, the gender of the client changes, and so does the whole mode of lawyer/client interaction. Although Maitland has been desperate to speak with his daughter, he suddenly makes her wait outside while he deals with his client. Rather than the non-realistic presentation of legal appointments that we have grown used to, the scene is realistic. And, rather than our protagonist's usual verbosity, he is quiet and attentive, listening to Maples and asking him questions that lead his client to fill out his story. This scene is so different in mode and ostensible subject matter that critics have been

Inadmissible Evidence

hard pressed to justify its presence. Hayman (1972, 100) sees it as an independent scene about police harassment of gay men, hardly a major theme in the rest of the play. It is unusual for a playwright to devote a lengthy scene to a new character that has no impact on the plot, so late in the play. But Maples provides further elaboration on major themes related to Maitland, and Maitland's interaction with Maples reveals a new and important facet of his character.

Maples is identified with Maitland in several ways. First, Maitland has been identified with sexual offenders from the start, from the judge's accusation in the first lines of the play (9), to the meeting with Bennet (36), through Hudson's opinion that Maitland should be the one to deal with Maples's case (74). Yet, the nature of Maples' sexual offense is kept from us until his scene, where we realize that, rather than being an act of violence, it is the story of a man who is entrapped by the police for homosexual activities, a man who admits to his guilt and faces imprisonment rather than imperil his ex-lover. What might have been a sordid story turns out to be one of romantic self-sacrifice. The story collapses any stereotyped opposition between casual sexual activity and ethical value that the audience might have. This is important, since it serves to soften any judgments we might be tempted to pass on Maitland's philandering.

Second, Maples, like Maitland, is afraid of "being found out." This fear was given special emphasis in the opening trial scene:

> BILL: [...]And then, I have always been afraid of being found out.
> JUDGE: Found out?
> BILL: Yes.
> JUDGE: Found out about what? (19)

The triple repetition of "found out," further intensified by the fact that Maitland never answers the Judge's question, leads us to wonder what he is concealing. He certainly has a lot he would like to conceal: professional misconduct, sexual infidelity, feelings of inadequacy. Maples provides the first echo of Maitland's phrase after the trial scene:

> I was terrified of getting into trouble or being found out in even little things, like not dubbing my football boots or never understanding what 'parsing' was. (95)

But the phrase "found out" has an even more sinister meaning for Maples, since being "found out" as a homosexual could lead to six month's imprisonment (75). Maples' monologue tells of his failed attempts to hide his secret; his disastrous marriage, made to conform to the expectations of others; his first anonymous sexual encounter; his preference to respond to, rather than initiate, sexual contact, in the dark, if possible; his clandestine seduction of a sales clerk in the unsuspecting presence of the clerk's wife. It is a story of the conflict between passion and pretense.

The story reflected in the progression of the scene itself. Maples begins by trying to pass, despite the legal charges and his own nature, as a stereotypical heterosexual male. He begins by talking about his wife and daughter, and his skill at sports. When he mentions a close school friend, he immediately adds that "We talked about girls constantly, all the time" (94). It is only with time that he can admit "I never liked girls" (96). Eventually, his conflicted feelings about himself emerge. He does not wish to undergo psychiatric treatment, "I want to be who I am (96), and yet feels guilty--"They're right to get me, people like me" (98). He wants to plead guilty, out of exhaustion. Like Maitland, he is being exhausted by the conflicts within himself.

But, even as Maitland is giving up on his own life, he insists that Maples not capitulate. He refuses to let Maples plead guilty, extracts more information from him, and finally decides to invent an eyewitness who will help exonerate Maples. This scene provides an alternate scenario to Maitland's. Rather than resign oneself, the play shows that it is possible, even important, to fight against both the social and personal *status quo*, even using methods expressly prohibited by the state. The inclusion of the Maples scene allows the play to encompass the alternatives of subversion and capitulation within its protagonist.

This challenge to the established order is expressed in a muted tone, however. Maples dominates the scene's language, and his tone is quiet. He lacks Maitland's dizzying shifts of focus and verbal inventiveness. His evasions, though clear, are less witty and hyperbolic. It carries some of the calm of the Mrs. Andersen scene, but with realism, rather than reverie, as its dominant register. The intensity of the manifestative qualities lessens, and a narrative sequence of events presents a tale of progressive alienation and weariness, love and betrayal.

The quiet realism of this scene gives way to Maitland's confrontation with Jane, a bravura set piece that recapitulates the entire emotional development of *Inadmissible Evidence*, from fear through anger and aggression, to regret and renunciation. Rather than entering and exiting the office, Jane is the only character revealed onstage in mid-scene, and disappearing in a blackout. Her silence throughout this long harangue, as well as her means of appearance, help mark this scene as the most highly stylized, after the comparative realism of Maples' scene. If Maples in the most fully characterized of Maitland's visitors, Jane is the least. Indeed, she can be said to be more an emblem of youth than a character.

The speech is an attempt at a formal *apologia*, a detailed explanation and defense of the causes of his suffering. There are few signs of fragmentation here; the statements develop and build in a highly rhetorical form. From the phone call at the beginning of this act, through his meetings with clients, Maitland has become less fragmented. Here, in his attempt to present his deepest feelings to an unresponsive interlocutor, Maitland forges strong linguistic links between his statements:

> You are unselfconscious, which I am not. You are without guilt, which I am not. Quite rightly. Of course, you are stuffed full of paltry relief for emergent countries, and marches and boycotts and rallies, you, you kink your innocent way along tirelessly to all that poetry and folk worship, *and* looking gay and touching and stylish all at the same time. But there isn't much loving in any of your kindness, Jane, not much kindness, not even cruelty, really in any of you, not much craving for the harm of others, perhaps just a very easy, controlled sharp, I mean "sharp" pleasure in discomfiture (106).

Here, the previously alternating impulses of aggression and longing for conciliation are represented simultaneously, intertwined within single sentences. Maitland sets himself apart from his daughter and her generation, but he describes her in such attractive terms ("gay and touching and stylish") and tries so desperately to establish contact with her, that we simultaneously perceive both his alienation and his attraction. This synthesis lays bare Maitland's most fundamental ambivalences in an eloquent and extended speech that serves as the climax of the entire play. Faced with the representative of a generation that seems to have lost its capacity for deep emotion, Maitland feels threatened. Jane becomes the representative of a modern mentality that can neither understand nor accept emotional intensity. Maitland is doomed to verbal exhaustion in this encounter, since Jane's silence evokes all of his deepest feelings, but offers no language or emotion in return. The verbal and emotional protagonist confronts his silent and passionless progeny, and no conversation between the two proves possible. By the end of the speech, Maitland has been drained of his anger and passionate longing. He sends her off, with a recognition that the future is hers:

> You know what God is supposed to have said, well in Sunday School anyway? God said, He said: Be fruitful and multiply and replenish the earth. And *subdue* it. It seems to me Jane, little Jane, you don't look little any longer, you are on your way at last, all, to doing all four of them. For the first time. Go on now (107).

If Osborne contrasted the need to persevere despite exhaustion in the Maples scene, here he presents another alternative, one totally Other to Maitland. Her youth is contrasted with his age, her emerging power to his growing helplessness, his verbosity to her silence, and his passion to her lack of it. Osborne chooses not to dramatize Jane, but to leave her as a symbolic presence, at the far limit of this presented world, without the subjectivity that so dominates its protagonist. Certainly, a feminist critique of *Inadmissible Evidence* could easily begin with Osborne's choice to withhold language from this key character.

After the scene with Jane, there is a brief exchange with Joy, and the final entrance of Liz. His aggression spent, he is withdrawn and hovering on the verge of silence. Maitland has been more candid and open with Liz than with any other character. He has repeated important passages from the dream trial in his conversations with her, thus establishing the great intimacy the two of them share. He admits to her alone that he has trouble remembering anything, and that he can cope with the effects of his headache only if he keeps his head upright and does not move about too rapidly. Only with Liz can he speak his thoughts openly and give full expression to his anxieties in a dialogue. Although he has attempted to be frank with Jane as well, his attempt

Inadmissible Evidence 53

to speak with her was a complete failure; she would not respond to him. His final dialogue is shared with Liz, and with her departure, Maitland resigns himself to solitude. She has been the only character able to understand the full complexity of his impulses. Through her, we are led to put Maitland's problems in perspective, after the huge magnitude established in his tirade. The problems need not be tragic, and the gently comic and affectionate tone of the scene presents a domestic alternative, in which confrontations need not be lacerating, and personal limitations need not be devastating. But the play has moved beyond the point where anything but solitude is imaginable for Maitland. With her exit, the only possibilities left for him are inauthentic conversation, pointless dispute, or silence. He chooses silence.

It is in this final scene that words first fail him. For a character of such unbridled virtuosity, these admissions of tenderness are particularly moving in their awkwardness:

> And I shall never forget your face or anything about you. It won't be possible. I think, I'm quite certain, not that it matters, I loved you more than anyone. (114-115)

The hesitation and simplicity of Maitland's vocabulary contrasts with his rhetorical brilliance, wit and virtuosity earlier in the play. His tendency to qualify his expressions is used to manifest vulnerability here, rather than frustration or scorn.

After Liz leaves, the only possible means of continuing dialogue is by telephone. That is far more attenuated, however, since we only hear half of the dialogue; Anna's presence is only defined by Maitland's words to her. Tenuous though it is, the phone conversation is Maitland's last connection with the world outside of his office. When he tells Anna that he will not come home, but will wait in his office, the final solo of the play reaches its conclusion.

Inadmissible Evidence is a series of stylistically diverse scenes, each of which is unified through its own set of contentions. The series is unified by recurring motifs and the presence of the protagonist. Its variety of styles has been attacked, but it is doubtful that the play could so fully present the complex nuances of a relatively static situation without the use of those devices. Here the playwright has found a successful alternative to creating variety through plot development.

Osborne is foremost a writer of dramatic language, rather than a contriver of plots. The most awkward features of his plays are his plot devices; Allison's miscarriage in *Look Back in Anger*, the native insurrection in *West of Suez*, the attack on the house in *Watch It Come Down*, and the blackmail plot in *A Patriot for Me* show dramatic coincidence and contrivance at its most unconvincing. *Inadmissible Evidence*'s structure avoids this weakness with plot, developing various facets of a situation with the barest skeleton of a causal sequence. The ultimate semantic context us Maitland's, and Ronald Hayman (1972, 103) has argued that the play fails to provide a critique of his viewpoint. I would argue, however, that the final scenes with Maples, Jane, and Liz do provide alternatives to the fatalistic self-destruction articulated by the rest of the play. Maitland's course of action is not inevitable. He himself prescribes other courses of action for those around him. Indeed, one might say that, for all of his problems, Maitland's withdrawal is never fully accounted for in realistic terms. It lacks an objective correlative. Whatever it was that Bill Maitland was afraid of being "found out" about never really is articulated. The silence at the play's end still holds a secret, beyond all its brilliant language.

In *Inadmissible Evidence*, the expressive qualities are dominated by the psychological state of its protagonist. The other characters are less complex and do not equal him in range or intensity. Everything focuses on a single figure who demands understanding and empathic response. Through highly disconnected speeches, repeatedly interrupted actions, and frequently emended and questioned assertions, we are led through an intensely emotional context which require we expend great mental energy following the play as it unfolds, an energy that is demanded in response to the virtuoso performance of the actor playing Maitland. As the implications of Maitland's situation grow clearer and the view of his situation less fragmented, the play becomes drained of its anxious energy and approaches a state of resigned exhaustion. This catharsis of the extralinguistic situation is mirrored by a movement from grammatical complexity and fragmentation to simplicity and silence.

Osborne's primary achievement of *Inadmissible Evidence* is in the drawing of Bill Maitland, a multifaceted character who can both dominate the action of a full-length play, and still carry secrets with him to the end. He has created a highly individualized yet representative figure, a bravura acting role with depth and insight, and a protagonist worthy of comparison with such novelistic prototypes of the existential anti-heroes as Dostoyevski's Underground Man and Camus' Mersault. Few roles in the modern British theatre offer such a fusion of virtuoso acting opportunities and stunning psychological acuity.

But Osborne is also to be admired for the world he has built up around that protagonist, where the truths about all the characters go beyond any simple judgments. The title of the play points to the insufficiency of the legal system, or any social system, to do justice to the full complexity of human beings and their relationships. Thus, Mrs. Garnsey, who divorces her husband because she cannot bear his isolation; Mrs. Tonks, with her depression; Mrs. Andersen with her painful lack of self-esteem; Maples, whose entrapment is the result of his love for another man who has already given him up; all the stories depend on deeply felt emotions that are not admissible in a court of law. Equally, Maitland's own trial cannot hope to be without its limitations. Complete knowledge, even self-knowledge, is impossible, and Osborne's drama here holds a compassion that withholds judgment. For there is more to be known about us than we are judged on, and that information may be inadmissible not only to those around us, but to ourselves.

THE SILENT RETREAT: "BINGO"

Unlike *Inadmissible Evidence*, which is impelled forward by the relentless verbal activity of its protagonist, Edward Bond's *Bingo* is dominated by a protagonist who tries to remain aloof and invulnerable. Beginning in silence and inaction, Bond's Shakespeare resists definition until events force him to recognize his moral responsibilities in the social world. He resists both the commitment of speech and the commitment of action. When events at last force him to speak, he reserves his deepest reflections for soliloquy, rather than public expression, and retreats from the realities he has been forced to confront by a second, more thorough retreat, that culminates in his suicide. For much of *Inadmissible Evidence*, Bill Maitland fears the absence of dialogue, preferring dispute to silence. Shakespeare prefers silence to the linguistic revelation of social realities. If a stage play depends on the manifestation of psychic states for much of its power and theatrical effect, as I have argued in the earlier chapters of this study, *Bingo* presents an interesting problem: is it possible to write an effective play about a character who tries to avoid manifesting his anxiety and despair, and actually avoids the situations in which those qualities might be brought to the surface?

At first glance, Shakespeare might appear to be a singularly uninteresting protagonist. The play begins with him consciously resisting verbal definition. He is onstage and silent for most of the first scene. Four times the side text states "Shakespeare doesn't react" (3), and this impassivity is further suggested by his many silences.

Silence has no meaning in itself. It is the absence of meaning units, the manifestation of either an inability to confer meaning or of a decision not to confer meaning. Silence cannot define itself. It is only given signification by the words that surround it, or by the actions that accompany it. The text can only endow silence with signification by nesting it within the structure of the text, much as Zen painters use their brush strokes to articulate the empty spaces of the scroll. In a theatrical performance, however, silence is not merely a description of a momentary pause in the delivery of the main text. It is also an action performed by a character. Rather than being just contextually determined by the text, the actor's silence is an action that manifests a decision to remain silent. An actor is always communicating something, constantly manifesting some qualities every moment s/he is onstage; his/her posture, facial expression, and movements communicate something to the spectator, however vaguely.

In the stage direction, "Shakespeare doesn't react," Bond is aiming at the histrionic equivalent of textually qualified silence. But the direction in the side text will be less neutral when an actor plays Shakespeare. Does the character not answer because he is preoccupied, traumatized, rude, senile, exhausted, or in ecstasy? This question is never directly answered by the text, though the ensuing action serves to limit a range of valid interpretations of his initial silence and inaction. Patrick Stewart, who played Shakespeare in two productions of *Bingo*, has noted the potential range of psychic states in the protagonist suggested by the text, from intellectual isolation to intense inquisitiveness (Hay & Roberts 1980, 188). In fact, as we shall see, Bond's dramaturgy in *Bingo*, as in most of his plays through *The Fool*, admits of great variety in interpretation.

The two parts of *Bingo* follow the same general pattern of development. Both begin with the silent and withdrawn protagonist being confronted with evidence of hatred, greed, brutality, and social injustice. The events elicit a deep response from him, but he cannot transfer his impulses to action or sustained dialogue. Instead, he lapses into monologue. His inability to sustain a verbal relationship is further underscored by his physical withdrawal from the other characters; he leaves his house for his garden, the gallows, the inn, the snow-covered fields, and finally returns home, locks himself in his room and takes poison.

If the figure of Shakespeare and his wishes determined the causal sequence of events in *Bingo*, there would be neither speech or dramatic action of any kind, only catatonic withdrawal. Fortunately, however, the play contains forces that manage to overcome the inertia exerted by its protagonist, and compel him to reveal both intellectual insights and manifestative qualities. In fact, we can say that *Bingo* succeeds to the extent that its protagonist fails in his attempted retreat.

Unlike Maitland, who is aware of the full extent of his dilemma from the very beginning of the play and defines not only his own semantic context but the context of the play as well, Shakespeare only gradually becomes aware of his social situation and responsibilities as external forces break down his reserve. Bond creates a world that is understood by us before the protagonist understands it. The discrepancy between the spectator's knowledge and the protagonist's creates an ironic distance that is only gradually bridged as Shakespeare undergoes his education.

The figure of the social innocent who slowly learns about the nature of human society through a series of dramatic episodes is a common figure in Bond's full-length works through *The Woman*. Len (*Saved*), Arthur (*Early Morning*), Kiro (*Narrow Road to the Deep North*), Lear (*Lear*), Willy (*The Sea*), John Clare (*The Fool*), and the General (*We Come to the River*) are all naive observers who gradually become aware of the dominant forces functioning in their societies. To the extent that they observe the presented world, these characters project assertions that guide our constitution of that world. But, insofar as they lack the omniscience and certain claim to truth that the third person narrator has in fiction. Their statements are interpreted, both against the world as it is described by other characters, by the world as it is defined by the side text (and, in production, through its physical aspects), and by the goals that they are pursuing through those acts of assertion. None of the characters in Bond's plays are able to stand outside of the presented world and comment on it with the instant authority of Gower in *Pericles* or the Stage Manager in *Our Town*. Bond's observers are themselves are elements within the social microcosm he constructs, shaped by its social dynamics, and are ultimately judged by the playwright according to the actions those characters perform to combat the evils they have witnessed.

Many of Bond's observers come to publicly condemn the social injustices they have witnessed. Lear, the General, and John Clare are observers who become social prophets. Shakespeare's behavior is far less exemplary. At first, he appear to evade the issue entirely. When the Old Woman tries to speak with him about enclosure, Shakespeare avoids the commitment of a definite statement:

> OLD WOMAN: They've hed a meetin'. They thought I
> ought-a arskt.
> SHAKESPEARE: I don't know anything.
> OLD WOMAN: What'll yo' do?
> SHAKESPEARE: There's plenty of time.
> OLD WOMAN: Start buildin' bridges when your feet git
> wet. (3-4)

This indecisiveness is revealed to be nothing but a pose. From the beginning of the play, Shakespeare has been sitting in the garden with a sheet of paper in his hand. Until late in the scene, no one refers to the sheet of paper, and only Shakespeare pays any attention to it. Bond's side text sets up a strong image; England's greatest dramatist, sitting in a garden, absorbed in something he has written. Because it is Shakespeare, the audience is inclined to assume that the page represents some great, creative work. It is only when the paper is handed to Combe that we realize what it is from Combe's verbal reaction to it; it is Shakespeare's conditions for agreeing with Combe on the issue of enclosure. It isn't art, it's commerce.

Combe is offering Shakespeare financial advantages for sitting in his garden and remaining inactive:

> Don't support the town or the tenants. When the council
> writes, ignore them. Be noncommittal or say you think
> nothing will come of it. Stay in your garden. (6)

Combe seems to offer Shakespeare a bourgeois idyll--financial security in return for domestic non-productivity--but Combe is actually paying Shakespeare to lie through his evasiveness and silence, and thus falsify his social relationships. Shakespeare is betraying his profession, since a poet is only a poet when s/he communicates with others through language. Thus, Shakespeare's silence and lack of social commitment are to be seen as a definite betrayal of his most fundamental responsibilities. Even though he offers the Young Girl alms and tries to shield her and the Old Man from the moral indignation of Judith and the Son, his major action in the scene, the agreement with Combe, shows him forging a pact with the landed interest that will hurt the very objects of his charity. The scene ends with him doing precisely what Combe wants; avoiding the issue of enclosure, even within his own household. When the Old Woman presses him as to what he plans to do about enclosure, he first lies, "Nothing's decided." "Has the shouting woken my wife? See if she's all right" (10). Shakespeare has begun to live a lie.

Bond communicates Shakespeare's particular mendacity by having his words avoid the questions or challenges set by others, such as his evasion of the Old Woman's questions, or by having the side text give him one action, and the main text another. In the second scene, he responds to the bell that has just stopped ringing with a poetic image "Bells love silence" (16), while he looks over his business agreement with Combe, and prepares to sign it. The main text is about art; the side text about money. Bond gives the disjuncture a slightly ironic tone here, since Shakespeare's aphorism about silence, is actually all-too-appropriate to his action. Shakespeare is signing himself to silence to buy the security he loves. This and other disjunctures make up a complex extralinguistic situation, even though the language of main text is often quite simple.

The structure of *Bingo* places Shakespeare at the center, present in every scene, and surrounds him with characters who are making claims on him: Combe, Judith, the Old Woman, the Young Woman, the Son, and Ben Jonson. Since each of the claims is in itself simple, Bond achieves complexity by overlapping the demands in each scene. In the first scene, Combe and the Old Woman try to influence Shakespeare's decision on enclosure, while the Young Woman asks for help from him. Rather than simply alternating the topics, Bond juxtaposes them. The Old Man and the Young Woman copulate in the orchard while Combe and Shakespeare discuss rents. The financial negotiations are interrupted by the entrance of the Son, who has just seen his father with the Young Woman. Shakespeare does not enter into the argument that follows, but he provides a structural center, since the two incidents are united by his presence. Like many of Bond's protagonists, Shakespeare is often a silent presence onstage, and the scenes that take place in his presence are important for what he learns from watching them. It is not until the end of the first act that Shakespeare articulates what he has learned from the story of the Young Girl's destruction and death, but it takes that much time before the speech seems justified, rather than facile rhetoric:

> What does it cost to stay alive? I'm stupefied at the suffering
> I've seen. The shapes huddled in misery that twitch away
> when you step over them. (26)

If Bond's protagonists are to learn about their societies, they must first observe them in action. They are, for Bond, ideal images of the theatrical spectator, growing more socially aware by attentive watching.

They often learn by watching seemingly disjointed elements and forging links of understanding between them. This theatrical juxtaposition of simple but strongly differentiated elements is one of Bond's most characteristic devices. The interaction among a number of these simple elements in a single scene can be extremely sophisticated. At the beginning of scene three of *Bingo*, the side text states that the body of the Young Woman is hanging on the gibbet. The horror aroused by that sight, however, does not dominate the entire scene. Downstage left, Shakespeare sits on a bench facing the audience, his back toward the gibbet. Silent and seemingly isolated from the scene, we do not know what he is thinking of, or why he is there. Joan and Jerome, two laborers, enter, look at the corpse for a moment, and begin to eat their lunches. Their light dialogue deals with food and sex:

> JEROME: Yont yo' 'ungry?
> JOAN: I got extra. I know hot weather allus give yo' an appetite.
> JEROME: Yo' pick your grub like a bud with a wart end on its beak.
> (*He puts his arm around her waist.*)
> JOAN: Hold your noise, boy. An' give over throwin' crumbs down the front a my dress. (21)

This is not situational discourse, since the speakers are not discussing their setting, yet the physical location specified in the side text substantially modifies our understanding of the main text. The gibbet and the brooding figure of Shakespeare throw the otherwise inconsequential main text into sharp relief. The laborers simultaneously reveal their callousness and their appreciation of simple physical pleasures and companionship, which contrasts with Shakespeare's deep alienation.

Bingo

As Joan feeds the birds at the foot of the gibbet, the tableau suggests a primal tension between life and death, between a pastoral ideal and civilized cruelty. Here, the expressive quality emerging from the scene is not identical with the manifestative qualities of either speaker's expressions; rather, the tension produced form the juxtaposition of the expressions, the corpse, and the staring figure of Shakespeare asks us to perceive the whole stage picture as a *Gestalt* that has indistinct conceptual meaning, but has a powerful evocative force.

This is only one of the passages in *Bingo* in which the expressive qualities of a text may move far beyond simple identification with the emotional state of the speaker. All discourse is dependent on its setting to some degree, and there extent to which the expressive qualities of the main text may be modified by the physical setting, as established explicitly in the main text, or implicitly by stage directions in the side text. To forget the physical setting of the presented world at any moment can lead to grave distortions in interpretation. The dominant expressive quality of a scene may very well not be a simple empathic relationship to a single character, but may more likely arise from a complex of manifested states and physical aspects of the scene. One cannot equate the manifestative qualities within a scene with the expressive quality of the whole.

Bond's penchant for striking juxtapositions has led him to experiment with speeches that are delivered simultaneously, most notably and effectively in his libretto for Hans Werner Henze's opera, *We Come to the River*. There, the musical form of this work allows the overlapping scenes to be composed as ensembles. It is much more difficult to overlap speeches in spoken drama, since even the most intelligent listeners cannot perform the necessary acts of meaning conferral on two simultaneously uttered speeches withot great difficulty. The success of these passages in performance depends on the insertion of judicious pauses and the highlighting of key words and phrases in each speech. The fourth scene of *Bingo* contrasts the struggles of the peasants with Jonson's amusingly inaccurate evocation of rural life, through speeches delivered simultaneously. While Combe tries to intimidate the peasants, Jonson fantasizes about a life in the country: he would "Charm fish from the water with a song" and "gather simple eggs" (36). The effect of this juxtaposition on Shakespeare is only completely clear in the following scene, when he soliloquizes on the writer's responsibility not to distance himself from social injustice:

> Only a god or a devil can write in other's men's blood, and
> not ask why they spilt it or what it cost. (43)

Notice how the technique of simultaneous delivery distances us from identification with any one of the characters in the tavern scene. The darkly comic tone of the simultaneous speeches comes, not from the manifestative qualities of either speaker, but from the disparity between the two; we react to Jonson's ignorance of the situation. Shakespeare's emotional reaction is deemphasized, since he is listening, not speaking. One of the challenges in staging Bond's plays is to bring visual focus to the silent observers. Shakespeare does not elaborate on what he has learned until the next scene, and even then, only in a highly generalized fashion, that does not draw explicit links between the speech and the previous scene. He never directly refers to Jonson, Combe, or the Son. He does not summon up the scene in the inn, merely delivers his conclusions, and leaves us to establish the link between the observation and the conclusion. Bond leaves us to observe first and draw our own conclusions, without using any character in the play to rid of the responsibility of interpretation.

Just as Bond creates an illusion of complexity by juxtaposing disjunct actions, he builds character by exposing one clear, simple facet at a time. At first, the Old Man's sexual exploitation of the Young Woman in the first scene relates thematically to the importance of money in all human relationships in this play, and establishes him as a less dangerous version of Shakespeare and Combe. Yet, in the following scene, the Old Man becomes a figure of pity when we learn that he has been a victim of impressment and has been mentally stunted by a blow on the head with the blunt end of an ax. Finally, the Old Man's concern for the Young Woman after her whipping and his desire to see her on last time after she has been hanged show that he is capable of a tenderness and simple humanity that his social and intellectual superiors lack. The character of the Old Man doesn't change. We merely constitute a sense of his character from a sequence of strong, simple, varied strokes over the course of several scenes.

The disparity between the function served by a single character may at times make the character difficult to constitute as a whole. The Son, for example, is an outraged and unsympathetic son in the first scene, a religious visionary in the third, and a revolutionary in the fourth. He is never all three of these things in the course of a single scene or speech. Indeed, his observation to Judith, "Even the sinner's innocent" (24), seems particularly out of keeping with his self-righteous moral rigor in the other scenes. The justification for the line seems to be that Bond wanted a foil for Judith's brittleness in Scene Three and used the Son, although he is generally an anti-establishment variation of Judith. The overall dramatic pattern can take precedence over character consistency in Bond.

Not only does Bond juxtapose disparate images and expressions, but he creates a generic tension between the historical and documentary elements in *Bingo* on the one hand, and the parabolic elements on the other. Cohn (1981, 185) has succinctly noted, "Bond's plays seek rational direction through the theatricalization of fable." The resultant alloy of realistic particularity and parabolic generality has led to critical confusion in the discussion of *Bingo*; it has been described both as "naturalistic" (Wolfensperger 1976, 15) and "overly allegorical" (Worthen 1975, 477). The events of the play are based on a historical fact: the historical Shakespeare did sign a document that placed him on the side of those moneyed and landed interests that favored the enclosure of common lands (Bond 1975, ix-x, xviii). To Bond, such indifference to the sufferings of the poor seems incredible in a playwright capable of the social insights of *King Lear*, and Bond is fascinated by Shakespeare's contradictory impulses of poetic vision and personal indifference. Awareness of such a contradiction, Bond argues in his preface to the play, must have driven the Bard to suicide:

> I'm like a man who looks down from a bridge at the place where an accident has happened. The road is wet, there's a skid mark, the car's wrecked, and a dead man lies by the road in a pool of blood. I can only put the various things together and say what probably happened. Orthodox critics usually assume that Shakespeare would have driven a car so well that he'd never had an accident. My account rather flatters Shakespeare. If he didn't end in the way shown in the play, then he was a reactionary blimp or some other fool. The only more charitable account is that he was unaware or senile (x).

The use of historical figures, such as Shakespeare, Judith, and Ben Jonson, the importance of the enclosure struggle as a historical event, and the scattered references to Henry VIII, Elizabeth I, the burning of the Globe Theatre, public executions, and bear-baiting, all serve to reinforce the realistic qualities of the play, and encourage us to identify persons, places and events with their historical referents (Elam 1980, 106-107).

There are other devices, however, that undermine or seriously qualify those signs that communicate historical realism. The language makes no attempt to capture the flavor of seventeenth century English. It is contemporary and colloquial. Bond's Jacobeans sound very similar to the Japanese, Victorians, and vaguely medieval figures that populate Bond's other plays. Sometimes the characters betray a disconcerting knowledge of late twentieth century commonplaces. For example, Judith describes her mother's mental condition to her father:

> JUDITH: I'll tell you why she stays in bed. She hides from you. She doesn't know who she is, or what she's supposed to do, or who she married. She's bewildered-- like so many of us!
> SHAKESPEARE: (*flatly*) Stop it, Judith. You speak so badly. Such banalities. So stale and ugly (18).

Shakespeare is correct. Judith does speak in banalities, but they are not facile observations on melancholia and black bile. They are the banalities of the early 1970's--one expects the terms "identity crisis,", "alienation," and "mid-life crisis" to suddenly drop from Judith's Jacobean lips. Similarly, Jonson seems to have absorbed enough cocktail-party-Freud to venture self-analysis:

> My life's been one long self-insult. It came on with puberty. (34)

Shakespeare's reference to "Women with shopping bags stepping over pools of blood (26)" is more likely to evoke images of supermarkets than the streets of seventeenth century Stratford. If Bond's intention had been a historical reconstruction, *Bingo* would have to be judged as an appallingly clumsy and sophomoric attempt. But those anachronistic touches in the main text momentarily annihilate the historical distance between us and the presented world, and force us to see that the events of *Bingo* are not isolated incidents in the past, but are expressions of a dilemma rooted in our common social being. The anachronisms contribute to the parabolic generality of *Bingo*, just as the historical references contribute to its realistic specificity. This tension is not a result of the intentions of the characters within the presented world. Judith does not consciously choose to be anachronistic. She is consistent within her world. It is Bond who disturbs us by presenting a world that contains anachronistic touches. The effect is produced, not by the presented intentionality of the speakers, but by the presenter of the fictive world.

The technique of juxtaposition applies to other aspects of the main text as well. Despite the social issues raised by the play, Bond does not adopt the language of the thesis drama, which is characterized by clear causal relationships, syntactical subordination, and a tendency toward compound-complex sentences. Only Combe uses that clear, simple style of facts and arguments. The immediate issue that he raises, enclosure, is obviously only the occasion for the presentation of more general themes. Combe quickly provides us with a skeletal description of the issues, so it can be accepted as the basis for the subsequent actions:

> We're going to enclose--stake out new fields the size of all
> our old pieces put together and shut them up behind hedges
> and ditches. Then we can farm in our own way. Tenants
> with long leases will be reallocated on new land. Squatters
> and small tenants on short leases will have to go: we shan't
> renew. That leaves you, and some others, who own rents,
> on the land. (5)

The facts are quickly established, and no Shavian conversations on capitalism ensue.

Combe's exposition is highly compressed, factual, and devoid of expressive qualities. His style of speech is well-suited to the rapid exposition of necessary information, and characterized Combe as a man for whom the preservation of a heartless and calculated *status quo* is the sole good. Therefore, Combe's style of speaking simultaneously establishes expository information and suggests the limitations of the speaker.

Combe's language stands in sharp contrast to the language spoken by the rest of the characters in the most of the play, which is a combination of sentence fragments and sentence clusters that lack syntactic subordination. Bond's stage speech, as well as his dramaturgy, is paratactic. Shakespeare's description of the bear-baiting is an excellent example of this. It is composed of simple sentences and sentence fragments, each unit projecting a simple concrete image. Modifiers are few. The vocabulary avoids all but the most common words. The only colors, for example, that are ever mentioned in Bond's speech are neutral colors and red; Bond's palette excludes rich hues just as his speeches eschew unfamiliar words or constructions and his plots avoid sentimental or sensually pleasurable motifs. The sentences bring vivid images together, without ever establishing explicit connections between them.

Some of Bond's most striking speeches use this technique of verbal montage:

> OLD WOMAN: Hev yo' yeard summat a while back? I yeard a noise, blowed if I yont. I yeard thunder in snow one toime. Toime I were a gal. They say I were a dazzler. That seem afore your father step into the world!--but I remember on it. (44)

The Old Woman's recollection of thunder and her beauty bear no thematic, causal, or motivic relationship to the rest of the play. Temporally removed, from the present action by the use of past tense, it further retreats from the present moment--"a while back," "one toime," "toime I were a gal," "afore your father." The discontinuity between her lyric recollections and the present situation is underscored by the fact that the sound that reminded her of thunder was actually the report of a gun which has killed her husband. The inappropriateness of her comment within the extralinguistic context invests her comments with an added poignancy. Although the speech repeatedly refers back to its speaker--the word "I" appears six times-- the repetition only refers the expressions back to their common speaker, and does not provide any causal links or syntactical subordination. The Old Woman's brief and simple expression of recollected beauty stands in contrast to the glacial hatred and solipsism of Judith, Jonson, and Shakespeare. It suggests a positive range of experience generally neglected by these characters. The word "dazzler," carrying connotations of bright light, contrasts with the physical darkness of this nocturnal scene, as well as the general dreariness of this drama of night, autumn, and frozen spring. Like Ferdinand's very similar line in John Webster's equally grim *The Duchess of Malfi*, "Cover her face: Mine eyes dazell. She di'd yong" (IV.ii.297). The intrusion of light and simple lyricism in the Old Woman's speech throws the play's violence into sharp relief, without ever trying to explain how such beauty can coexist in the world with such cruelty.

These verbal disjunctions are used with particular force in the evocation of one of Bond's favorite themes--violence. For him, he has explained, violence is as inevitable a subject for him as manners were for Jane Austen (Bond 1972, v). In the following speech, the clipped, concrete images follow one another as so many boxer's blows:

> Flesh and blood. Strips of skin. Teeth scrapping bone. The bear will crush one of the skulls. Big feet slithering in dog's brain. Round the stake. On and on. The key in the warder's pocket. Howls. Roars. Men baiting their beast (25).

This speech is typical of Bond's verbal treatment of violence, one that differs fundamentally from its treatment in Senecan drama, opera, nineteenth century melodrama, and most English Renaissance drama. These other forms describe violent acts in a highly rhetorical fashion, matching the extravagance of the deed with extravagant language, as in Theremène's report of Hyppolyte's death in *Phèdre*, or Marcus' discovery of Lavinia, raped and mutilated, in *Titus Andronicus*:

> Speak, gentle niece. What stern ungentle hands
> Have lopp'd and hew'd and made thy body bare
> Of her two branches, those sweet ornaments,
> Whose circling shadows kings have sought to sleep in,
> And might not gain so great a happiness
> As half thy love? (II.iv.16-21)

At its most skillful, this traditional fusion of high style and violent description can create a highly charged emotional atmosphere, almost hysterical in its carefully calculated excesses. At its worst, it leads to bombast and bathos. Bond, on the other hand, strips away any rhetorical decoration in his descriptions of violence. There are no adverbs and few adjectives in the description of the bear-baiting, no words but the most familiar, and no words that call attention to

Shakespeare's personal feelings about the bear-baiting. The emphasis is placed on the scene that it is summoning up, not on the speaker's personal reactions. The style is clipped, concrete, and engenders revulsion and horror through physical description rather than apostrophe, superlatives, or figurative language. The diction is never allowed to soften, transform, or detract from the simple and horrible fact of gratuitous human brutality.

Shakespeare's education is impelled forward by his exposure to the brutality around him. He is, understandably, an unwilling student, whose desire to retreat is continually checked by his inability not to be totally oblivious to the pain and cruelty around him. But his introverted tendencies work to pull the play away from strong emotional confrontations, in which major characters qualify and challenge each others contexts. Shakespeare avoids disputatious situations that might allow manifestative qualities to emerge.

When he does speak, he uses the imagery of ice, metal, and death to describe his perceptions, images that suggest his coldness and inability to feel deeply or passionately about anything. Even his hatred, commonly considered a passionate emotion, has congealed:

> Don't be angry because I hate you Judith. My hatred isn't angry. It's cold and formal. I wouldn't harm you. I'll help you, give my life for you--all in hatred. (42)

The striking effect of this speech derives from the tension between the conventionally accepted notion of hatred as a passionate, "hot" emotion. Not only does Shakespeare describe his hatred as "cold", drawing on two meaning carried by the word, "unemotional" and "of low temperature," but his short, simple, and grammatically well-formed sentences exhibit no emotional intensity. The speech develops from cold hatred to a troubling generosity. Starting with the disturbing action of a father telling his daughter how much he hates her, the qualities lighten somewhat as he first says he would not harm her and then positively stressed what he *would* do for her, the two offers mounting in intensity ("I'll help you, give my life for you"). Having reached this climax of generosity, we are led back to an expression of his hatred. The first apparent contradiction, hatred without anger, has been replaced by an even more audacious contradiction, hatred that does not preclude self-sacrifice. The intellectual tension generated by the contradictions substitutes for the intense emotion that we might expect to see manifested in this situation, which becomes all the more disturbing by its absence. Frustrated audience expectations provide an insight into the frustrated and somewhat paradoxical emotions of Shakespeare and Judith.

The play would congeal around the frozen heart of its protagonist if Bond did not surround Shakespeare with vivid situations and characters who react to his coldness emotionally. Judith, the Son, and Jonson all provide passionate foils for the depressed and withdrawn protagonist. Judith repeatedly tries to provoke her father to dispute, and his silent response proves more aggressive than any verbal onslaught could be. Participation in a dispute, no matter how cruel, at least reveals a common linguistic ground and a set of common concerns. Instead of manifesting aggressive impulses by pitting speech against speech, Bond opposes verbal aggression against willful silence.

Shakespeare's silence is also strengthened by the opposition of his violent and incoherently expressive wife, who is heard sobbing and clawing the paint off the door with her nails. She has abandoned language altogether, and relies completely on frenzied indications of extreme frustration. Once again, Shakespeare's silence is dramatically interesting because it is colored by the passionate forces that try to force it to yield.

Ben Jonson's hatred is the antithesis of Shakespeare's congealed emotion. It reinforces our traditional view of the manifestative qualities associated with that emotion:

> Shall I tell you something about me? I hate. Yes--isn't that interesting? I keep it well hidden but its true: I hate. A short hard word. Begins with a hiss and ends with a spit: hate. To say it you open your mouth as if you're bringing up: hate. I hate you, for example. (33)

The compulsive repetition of the word "hate" at the end of the sentences, the ugliness of the imagery, and the tendency for the expressions to degenerate into sentence fragments, exhibit hatred in a more familiar and, therefore, less disturbing, manner. By describing the pronunciation of the world "hate" with such detail and perverse relish, the sound of the word takes on physically repulsive connotations. Bond foregrounds the sound of the word itself and suggests its appropriateness for the state it denotes. The fact that Shakespeare does not respond to this verbal aggression manifests an undefined mixture of indifference and inebriation. Jonson, however, is a close literary relative of Osborne's splenetic monologists, and does not require any encouragement from his interlocutor.

Jonson's monologizing, though different from Shakespeare's in emotional tonality, exhibits a similar self-absorption. Even when comes to understand the implications of his complicitous silence, Shakespeare's understanding remains incomplete because he is unable to share it with others. His deepest reflections are monologic. Linguistically stillborn, his ideas are not proclaimed to the world. The images of his monologue reveal a barren landscape of solipsism and spiritual death:

> If I wasn't dead I could kill myself. What is the ice inside me? The plague is hot--this is so cold. The truth means nothing when you hate. Was anything done? Was anything done? I sit in a wound as large as a valley. The sides are smooth and cold and grey. I sit at the bottom and cry at my own death. (43)

This speech is embarrassingly self-conscious in its cheap pathos and pseudo-profundity. "If I wasn't dead I could kill myself" exemplifies pretensions of despair writhing with existential chic. It would be wrong to label Bond a cheap and sentimental dramatist, however. He has found an appropriate language for Bond's Shakespeare, a representative of bourgeois self-absorption. Having ignored social realities and his personal responsibilities, Shakespeare finds himself in the ultimate desolation of his own habitual egocentrism. He even pretends to soliloquize in the presence of others, pretending to have renounced communication while he is indulging in it. "I talk to myself now," he mutters, "I know no one will ever listen" (26). Shakespeare projects his realizations through speech, but his self-indulgent means of projecting those insights reveal his inability to objectify his experience or transform it into positive action and concern for others.

But this is a dangerous strategy for a playwright, and can easily backfire. The passage quoted above contains an insight that Bond wants us to accept ("The truth means nothing when you hate") but is put in such a self-pitying context that we are more inclined to squirm at the manifestative quality of the speech than embrace the moral. Bond is a master at using self-absorption for comic effect, as in Jonson's pastoral yearnings, but less assured at its power to generate pathos. By having Shakespeare describe his feelings, rather than letting his feelings manifest themselves through the discussion of what he has observed, Bond turns the spotlight too brightly on what turns out to be the character's preoccupation with himself.

Bond is more successful in balancing social vision and manifestative quality in Shakespeare's climactic speech. Here, he finally fuses Combe's clarity with the play's strong imagery to make a statement that has no trace of maudlin self-concern:

> I howled when they suffered, but they were whipped and hanged so I could be free. That is the right question: not why did I sign one piece of paper?--no, no, even when I sat at my table, when I put on my clothes, I was a hangman's assistant, a gaoler's errand boy [. . .] (48).

The assertions are no longer about how the speaker feels, but how the speaker understands what he has done. Action, not emotion for its own sake, is the issue.

It is important to note, however, that even this final judgment of his social irresponsibility goes unheeded by the Son, who is lost in thoughts of his own. And even his death goes unnoticed. Those critics who would like to see *Bingo* as smoething other than an expression of despair (Hay & Roberts, 189-90; Worth 1981, 215) tend to avoid the fact that Shakespeare's social education leads him into even greater self-absorption and incapacity to help others than before.

Bond's theatrical juxtapositions can be considered his stylistic signature, as well as the key to an understanding of his artistic vision. This vision is presented in simultaneous, concrete, austere, and contrasting images, in which the various elements do not melt together into a harmonious whole, but exist within the same space without establishing an explicit relationship to each other. This explains the theatrical power of Bond's language and stage images, but also explains why the intellectual arguments of his dramas are somewhat blurred. Bond avoids the intellectual and rhetorical fireworks of George Bernard Shaw or the subtle, leisurely arguments of Harley Granville-Barker. The effect of his main text is generally far more dependent on the stage picture for its meaning and expressive quality to emerge.

Bond's strategies of disjunction are not without their peril to interpreters. They confront us with an emotional force born of dislocation, but sometimes the "rational" links that Bond wants us to forge remain unclear. We are invited to reconcile the disparate elements, but these poetic techniques do not necessarily lend themselves to rational resolution. Shakespeare contrasts the ugliness of bear-baiting and the beauty of the river, but the contrast is completely emotional and devoid of intellectual content. The final images of *Narrow Road to the Deep North* are undeniably powerful but have elicited convincing and opposing interpretations from careful critics (Worthen 1975, 466-479; Durbach1975, 486-87). With *Bingo*, critics have been tempted to fill in the fragments through recourse to Bond's own statements on the play and earlier drafts (Hay & Roberts 1980, 180-199), or through an invocation of Shakespeare's literary achievement (Worth 1981, 214-15). Both readings tend to mitigate the bleakness of the play as it is written. James C. Bulman (1986, 68) is much closer to the point when he argues, that for all Bond's professed abhorrence of the Theatre of the Absurd, *Bingo* is surprisingly close in tonality to *Endgame* and *Krapp's Last Tape*. Bond stresses the rational component of his theatre in his prefaces, but his most powerful theatrical images contain ciolent disjunctions that cannot be resolved through intellectual argument.

In fact, Bond's use of violent, disjunctive images, has had an unfortunate effect on some critics, who see all onstage violence as an indication of an affinity with the works of Antonin Artaud, or as proof of Artaudian influence (Stoll 1977, 161-81; Mander 1969, 37-38).The differences between Artaud's use of cruelty and Bond's are both stylistic and philosophical. For Artaud (1958, 79) cruelty is a metaphysical concept that conveys human vulnerability in the face of a inscrutable and seemingly hostile universe. Bond's images of cruelty are depictions of human callousness and injustice, products of social volition. Artaud is a visionary; Bond is a moralist. Artaud's theatre is one of transcendence, in which language becomes incantation to communicate mystical insights to the audience (Artaud 1958, 107-9). Bond's language avoids the rhapsodic and incantatory, and does not aim at whipping its audience into a frenzy. "Art," Bond has written:

can never commit itself to despair or the irrational. Art is
the human being claiming a rational relationship to the
world, perhaps especially when what it portrays might have
otherwise seemed absurd or tragic (1976, xvi).

Nothing could be further removed from Artaud's vision of the theatre as plague. Bond acts his spectator to act rationally, even in the face of irrationality.

This presents a great challenge for the spectator, since Bond's images of an irrational and violent world threaten to overwhelm both audience and character. Often Bond's observers are destroyed by their education, as they go insane, blind, or die. Shakespeare us so overwhelmed with the cruelty he sees that he withdraws into suicide. The balance between rationality and irrationality in Bond's plays is precarious, and often tilts in the direction of irrationality, for all the author's programmatic statements.

Bond's dramatic method differs from Osborne's in that Osborne is interested in empathic involvement with his characters as a primary aesthetic value, while Bond subordinates the emotional life of his characters to a social vision. In Bond, we are moved by our contemplation of the entire situation, rather than what a single, exceptional character feels. The range of manifested emotions in *Bingo* is far narrower that in *Inadmissible Evidence*, the expressions of emotion are less flamboyant, and the expressive qualities of the scene do not closely correspond with the manifestative qualities of the protagonist's speeches. Rather than using devices to emphasize the psychic states of his characters, Bond strips the language of rhetorical flourishes and forces us to contemplate the effects of human cruelty and injustice instead of the passions that might motivate that cruelty. The images of suffering that Bond chooses are so intense that they compensate for the relative lack of manifested passion in many of his major characters. The aesthetic force of *Bingo*, then, illustrates that manifestative qualities are not the only aesthetically valent qualities that can create expressive values in a drama, and that the manifestative qualities can even be deemphasized to allow the emergence of other expressive qualities.

HEARING A NAME: "VÉRA BAXTER"

Inadmissible Evidence begins with the protagonist onstage and his name proclaimed by the clerk, "William Henry Maitland" (9). *Bingo* begins with the protagonist sitting in silence, seemingly oblivious to the action around him. Marguerite Duras' *Véra Baxter, or, The Atlantic Beaches* begins with the protagonist offstage, the object of speculation and indirect assertions. "Non..." the bartender says over the phone to some unknown interlocutor as the main text begins, "Non...elle n'est pas encore rentrèe...non personne" (Duras 1980, 8) [No...she hasn't come back yet...no, nobody (Duras 1986, 21)]. Véra first makes her presence felt in the play as a pronoun with no antecedent, in a state of affairs in which her only predicate is absence. We will not see her until the third scene of the play. Until then, she is constituted through a series of assertions marked by evasiveness and lies, and punctuated with frequent silences.

Véra's absence should come as no surprise to us. The wives of both Osborne's and Bond's protagonists are extremely marginalized presences. Anna has a name, but little else; we only know her through Maitland's expressions concerning her and the words she addresses to her husband over the phone, which we never hear. Shakespeare's wife has neither a name nor, it seems, the ability to speak. Crying, banging, and scraping are the only indications of her presence in the presented world. Later in this study, we will meet the General's Wife in *The Hunting Party* and Quitt's Wife in *The Irrational Are Dying Out*, and hear John Greed in *Prelude to Death in Venice* talk to his nameless mother. Women in all of these plays are primarily appendages, foils to the protagonist, lacking names and stories of their own.

In *Véra Baxter* Duras focuses on the marginalization of women that is taken for granted in the works by these male playwrights and investigates that status. Véra's story emerges gradually and ambiguously, despite the forces that militate against the telling of her story.

Duras' texts often exist as generic mixtures, hybrids of play and novel, *recit* and screenplay. The text of *Véra Baxter* is partly the scenario of a screenplay, entitled *Baxter, Véra Baxter*, which, with the elimination of much of the side text (as Duras herself recommends in the preface to the volume) is also a stage play. For the purposes of this study, I am limiting my analysis to the main text, along with those indications of sound and silence that exist in the side text.

The play begins one afternoon in the bar of a hotel. There are three men there; the Bartender, Michel Cayre, and an anonymous customer. We hear the Bartender informing a caller of "her" absence, and then a series of states of affairs are projected, which concern Véra, but do not make her the object of the expressions: the location of the caller, the story of a house. "She" seems to be in the house, but is not answering the phone. Whereas "he" calls, "she" doesn't even answer the phone. "He" is active, speaking; "she" is passive, silent, out of reach.

The language is fragmentary, elliptical. The first eight lines of the play identify no one by name. There are as many sentence fragments as sentences. "Pause" is a frequent direction in the side text. Exposition is sketchy. We are not told the name of the couple who own The Colonnades, nor are we told their story in any detail. We are only told that "il y a eu une historie" (11) [something happened, once (21)] and now they rent the house out. The states of affairs are projected with great vagueness, preparing us for a play that will unfold gradually, suggestively.

The Customer, we learn, is like us; he does not know the story. He asks the question we want to know about this "She"--"Comment s'appelle-t-elle" (11) [What's her name? (21)]. The Bartender replies, through a series of assertions that convey the resistance to Véra even having an identity, let alone a story:

Baxter. Véra Baxter. [side text] Il y a dix ans qu'ils viennent l'été ici. Lui, c'est un promoteur, Jean Baxter...Vous n'avez pas entendu parler? (11, 12)	Baxter. Véra Baxter. They've been coming here for ten years now. He's in promotional work. Jean Baxter...You've never heard of him? (21)

The Bartender first answers the Customer by merely giving him Véra's last name, the part of her name that she takes from her husband. He then adds her first name, followed by a repetition of her married name. Once her name is mentioned, she begins to disappear from the Bartender's speech. She becomes subsumed into the collective "ils", and then disappears altogether as he changes the subject to her husband, Jean. The Bartender has things to say about Jean, but nothing, it would seem, about Véra. "Lui, c'est un journaliste, Michel Cayre" (12) [*He's* a reporter. Michel Cayre (21)], the Bartender identifies Michel to the Customer. Men are easily identifiable in the world of *Véra Baxter*; they are identified by their jobs. The women lack that tag.

Immediately after Michel is introduced, a woman walks into the bar. The side text identifies her to the reader as Monique Combès, but the audience is given no such information. She is nameless, and, for a moment, we might think that she *is* Véra, since we have not been told about any other female character. We realize, however, that this woman is not Véra, as she enters into a whispered conversation about the house, "elle," and Jean Baxter. Véra has dwindled back into pronominal status, but, since we are no longer total outsiders to the story, we are now able to follow the references.

The unknown woman, who only identifies herself as "une amie de Jean Baxter" (17) [a friend of Jean Baxter's (23)], apparently a euphemism for that almost archetypal role in bourgeois drama, the mistress of the married man, is identified, like Véra, through her association with a man. She is the agent of Jean in this scene. She knows that he has already bought the house that Véra is considering buying, that he knows that Michel Cayre is there with Véra, and that there is a "convention" (18), [agreement (23)] as yet undefined for us, between the two men that Michel is on the verge of violating. As she approaches the topic of this agreement, she hesitates, and is unable to finish three sentences that would further define the terms. This builds up suspense, as manifestative qualities point to the agitation with which the subject is broached, and constitutes the agreement as an "enigma" in the plot, an element in what Roland Barthes (1974, 19) referred to as the "hermeneutic code" of the text, which encodes questions about the presented world that we are led to desire answers to.

But we are not to have our curiosity satisfied for some time. Michel responds in words that underscore the mystery:

MICHEL: Vous voulez dire: la succession de mensonges qui entoure Véra Baxter.	MICHEL: You mean: the series of lies surrounding Véra Baxter.
M. COMBES: (*nette*) Oui. (18)	M. COMBES: (*Frank.*) Yes. (*Pause.*)(23)

The agreement grows more sinister; it is now a series of lies. The enigma grows even more intriguing, as Duras dangles the possibility of hidden transgressions before us. Yet she warns us to consider everything we hear from now on painstakingly; this is a story about lies. The story of Véra is now doubly difficult: both through the difficulty of telling any woman's story in the first place, and through the difficulty of separating truth from falsehood in the story of this particular one.

Questions of truth and falsehood become explicitly foregrounded as Monique and Michel turn to the Customer, the silent witness of the previous conversation, and asks him what he thinks. The situation suddenly takes on a metadramatic dimension as the characters address a spectator on the course of the play. No longer an invulnerable observer, free to enjoy his voyeuristic status silently, he is brought into the action and challenged. Duras challenges us through the challenge to the Customer, asking us to account for the role we play in the constitution of the presented world.

His response continues the metadrama: "Que l'illusion devrait rester entière" (20) [That the illusion should remain total (23)]. On the level of discourse within the presented world, this means one thing; that the lies surrounding Véra should not be violated. To us, as an audience, it means another. He is asking the theatrical illusion remain complete; not opened to include him. The Customer's anxiety is manifested here as he crosses over the line from observer to participant. He hesitates; his speeches are marked with ellipsis marks as he tries to articulate his understanding of the situation he has been observing, in which the lies may exist to protect some kind of truth. He deepens the idea of lies by suggesting a paradoxical situation in which lies might exist to protect the truth, qualifying their totally sinister and negative connotations. He almost stammers out this insight, and then turns to the other characters for confirmation, only to be greeted with slience. We, like the Customer, will have to test the validity of his tentative hypothesis for ourselves.

To the last, however, he tries to keep himself distant from the play. "C'est ce qui apparaît de l'extérieur" (20) [Or so it seems from the outside... (23)], as if he could remove himself from the presented world once he had entered into it. But there is no possible "outside" that the observer can occupy with impunity. Duras encodes the roles of spectatorship within the work, so it can be investigated, not only in *Véra Baxter*, but in *L'Amante anglaise,The Malady of Death, Savannah Bay,* and *The Atlantic Man* (Willis 1987, 151). The story of *Véra Baxter* is one in which the person who begins only as a name and the person who hears the name gradually work their way toward a meeting.

The second scene, still set in the bar, further develops Véra's elusiveness, her inability to become a stable, known signifier in anyone's speech. We never hear her name spoken in this scene, just third-person pronouns. The scene begins with Michel telling Monique how he had mistaken her for Véra at their first meeting, simply because she was in the company of Jean. This recollected mistake echoes back to our uncertainty upon Monique's entrance in the first scene. Véra can be quite transparent, it seems. "On la voit quand elle est sans lui" (24) [You notice her when she's not with him (24)] observes Michel, leading us to infer that, in her husband's presence, you don't notice her. Monique takes this even further, suggesting that, once you've seen her with her husband, you never notice her. Michel hesitates to agree with that. Monique, the mistress, works to efface Véra's presence by strengthening Jean's; while Michel, the lover, resists that annihilation. The degree to which Véra exists in this scene is at the mercy of the descriptions of her, as she is defined, or undefined, in the power differentials between husband, mistress, and lover.

Monique leaves, and the Customer is further implicated in the story. Michel comes and sits at his table, and explains his dilemma.

He's going to leave "her," he explains in broken phrases. He's in pain, but the source of the pain remains unfocused. He can describe "her" by describing her relationship to her rich, philandering husband, but can say little about her directly. When he does not define her in relationship to her husband, he defines her as the object of his understanding, or, more appropriately, of his lack of understanding:

> MICHEL: Je l'ai perdue. Je ne sais pas quand. Je ne sais pas quand. Je n'arrive pas á savoir... (*temps*)...ni pourquoi j'y tiens... (29)
>
> MICHEL: I've lost her. I don't know when it happened. I can't seem to figure it out. (*Pause*.)...I don't know why I want to know... (25)

Véra is defined, paradoxically, by further lack of definition. Michel does not know her; he says he's "lost" her, but does not even know when that happened. The piling up of expressions about Véra merely intensifies our sense of distance from her; her Otherness is reiterated.

While Michel's language disintegrates, the Customer's gains in precision and direction. No longer hesitant, he asks simple questions and makes simple statements when Michel lapses into silence, encouraging him to continue the story. He suggests possibilities that Michel has not entertained. While Michel offers the word "docilité" (31) [docility (25)] as a possible reason for Véra staying sequestered at The Colonnades, the Customer surprises Michel with the alternative that it might be "certitude" (31) [conviction (25)]. The Customer is beginning to work toward a version of the truth that transcends the accounts of the characters involved in the story.

The sense of crisis builds throughout this scene. In the first decision we see anyone make in the play, Michel decides he must leave Véra. Véra, for reasons we do not understand, stays in the house. Above all, we learn that Jean Baxter, who has left his wife for months on end, we learn at the end of the scene, is suddenly calling every fifteen minutes to find out how she is.

The expressions increasingly point to a crisis throughout this scene, and yet the style remains cool. Anxiety and depression are indicated through sentence fragments and ellipsis marks, while the vocabulary remains simple. There are no words of physical description, no expletives, no exclamation points, no metaphors, no similes, no figures of speech. The verbs are usually simple and colorless. The states of affairs primarily pertain to states of mind and motivation, rather than objects in the world. Just as the we observe the main characters in locales that are foreign to them (Papin 1988, 19-20) and removed from their personal surroundings (a bar, a house for rent), so too, we feel a removal from the clutter and complexity of our daily lived experience. The clutter that was so much a part of *Inadmissible Evidence* is absent here. While Osborne seems incapable of imagining such distance, and Bond criticizes distance and self-absorption as socially derelict, Duras takes it as an inescapable given of human experience. In its simplicity of language and strong interior focus, *Véra Baxter* is a unique contribution to the French tradition of outwardly restrained, internally agonized drama, the drama of Racine, Musset, Mauriac and Gabriel Marcel.

With the third scene, the setting moves to The Colonnades, and we are finally presented to Véra. Having had her enigmatic nature built up for two scenes, we are eager to see if we can understand her any better than Michel. Her first lines, spoken from offstage, however, seem bereft of mystery. She shows Monique the house, and chatters about the children, the house and her husband. The language is casual, impersonal; that of a stereotypical, middle-class wife and mother.

The tone abruptly shifts, however, with the offstage sounds of the "Turbulence," as Duras labels it in the side text. The Turbulence is a sound effect, of mixed laughter, shouts, and dance music, that punctuate the main text of *Véra Baxter*. We first heard it during the opening scene, at the first mention of The Colonnades. It then reappeared after Customer offered his tentative explanation as to why the illusions built around Véra should not be destroyed. From now to the end of the play, it is given a realistic motivation; it is the sound coming from a party at a nearby house. But it is not handled as a realistic device. The Turbulence intrudes violently one moment, only to completely fade away the next. A set of indications coming from an anonymous and physically removed mass, it is not given any precise definition, but it does render the isolation of the protagonist more palpable. When we first heard it, it punctuated the announcement of where Véra was; the second time, it questioned the Customer's hypothesis "ironique" (20) [ironically (23)], and prompted him to qualify it. Now, it is linked to Véra's state of mind by its juxtaposition to the main text:

Au loin, le bruit de la turbulence a repris. Turbulence: danses, rires et cris. VÉRA: Des voyous, peut-être, qui sont entrés.(*temps*) Il paraît que les villas sont visitées l'hiver, des gens entrent... Silence. M. COMBES: (*temps*) C'est une fête, on dirait. [...] VÉRA: C'est tellement isolé ici...On dirait la Californie... on crierait...personne ne vous entendrait. (35, 36)	(*Far away, the sounds of the TURBULENCE have started up again. Dancing, laughter and screams.*) VÉRA: Vandals who've broken in, perhaps. (*Pause.*) Apparently, the houses here are raided during the winter, people break in...(*Silence.*) M. COMBES: (*Pause.*) There seems to be a party. (*Silence.*) VÉRA: It's so isolated here...you'd think you were in California...if you screamed...no one would hear you. (26)

Véra's first reaction to the Turbulence is one of anxiety; she characterizes the sound is one of invaders. Her solitude having been invaded by Monique, a mistress and agent of her husband's, the sound of the Turbulence is enough to move Véra from small talk to a manifestation of more personal feelings. Monique dismisses the sounds as those of a party, minimizing any threat.

Once the Turbulence dies away, however, Véra reacts every bit as fearfully to the silence. She sees the presence of outsiders as a threat, and then sees isolation as a threat. This desperate impasse, however, is quickly effaced by a return to domestic chat. The Turbulence is able to effect a rupture, however temporarily, in her superficial conversation, allowing the clear manifestation of a psychic state to emerge briefly

Yet Véra is no more capable of telling her story to Monique than Michel was able to tell it to the Customer. Adulterous wife and mistress warily circle around each other, trying to figure out how much the other knows. Even when Monique confronts Véra with the fact that she knows about her liaison, Véra's response is remote, even indifferent:

Ça s'est trouvé comme ça, jour après jour. Je n'ai rien voulu de pareil. (42)	It just happened; one day, then another, I didn't want anything like that to happen. (27)

There is no apparent passion, shame, or defensiveness in her reply. The very flatness of the reply renders Véra's emotional involvement in the affair opaque. Duras thus continues to sustain the enigmas constructed about the figure of Véra Baxter, but she does so at the risk of depriving the scene of emotional life. Neither character is actively pursuing an objective; it is never clear what either Monique or Véra stand to gain through their transactions. The scene's action is less the interaction of the two women than a dialogue in which, haltingly, circuitously, and ambiguously, Véra's voice begins to turn toward the telling of her tale, the tale no one else has been able to tell. Monique encourages the forward rhetorical process of Véra with statements of her own and quotations from Jean.

In this scene, Véra moves from the persona of the bourgeois wife and mother, who is about to discuss the summer home with her spouse, to the woman who is waiting for her husband to call so she can tell him about her lover. Monique gently challenges Véra's bland and hesitant assertions. When Véra tells how her affair with Michel began, Monique replies:

Véra, c'est faux ce que tu racontes là, n'est-ce pas? (46)	Véra, you're not telling the truth, are you? (28)

But the challenge never develops into a dispute:

VÉRA: (temps) Oui.
M. COMBES: [side text]
    On ment beaucoup
    toi et moi.
VÉRA: Beaucoup.
    Oui.(46-47)
	VÉRA: (Pause.) No.
	M. COMBES: Both you
	    and I lie a lot.
	
	VÉRA: A lot. Yes. (28)

Monique never directly challenges a particular of Véra's tale; in fact, it is impossible to tell what has motivated Monique's question. In the pause after the question, there is a moment of tension, which is dissipated somewhat as Véra admits she has been lying. Monique does not, however, does not follow this up and ask for a true version of the events, which could then provoke either a dispute or a clarification of the exposition. Rather, she projects a state of affairs that links Véra and her, changing the subject. Her question makes us doubt Véra's expressions, without giving us any specific thing to doubt. The "conspiracy of lies" has grown to include the protagonist, but the nature of that conspiracy, which none of the characters seem at all interested in discovering, remains indistinct.

In contrast to the lies, Monique builds toward two revelations of truth near the end of the scene. After discussing Jean with Véra, she remarks on his distance, which seems an inability to love, but then, she says, after a long pause:

> Quelquefois, on découvre   Sometimes, you discover
> la vérité. (53)   the truth (29)

The Customer had earlier posed the hypothesis that lies might exist to protect a truth. Now, Monique is putting forth something as a truth. In this play of lies and enigmas, we have come to desire clarification. Now, it seems, we are going to get some.

Duras builds the suspense to Monique's revelation:

> VÉRA: Quand?   VÉRA: When?
> M. COMBES: Hier,   M. COMBES: Yesterday,
>   quand il a téléphoné   when he called to
>   pour savoir où tu   find out where you
>   étais. (53)   were. (30)

The revelation is, like almost everything else in the play, indirect. The philandering Baxter calling to find out where his wife is a truth that runs counter to his long absences from her and his seeming inability to love. The revelation is a revelation of personal emotion, not witnessed, not even reported, but inferred. Once again, the impact of the revelation is muted by the interlocutor's lack of a strong and specific reaction to it:

> VÉRA: [side text] Je   VÉRA: I thought it would
> pensais que ça durerait   last forever. (*Long pause.*)

toujours. (*temps long*)　　　That wouldn't have been
(*Deuxième fois*) Ça n'aura　possible. (30)
pas été possible. (53)

The object of this remark is unclear. Is it her love for Jean? Jean's for her? Hers for Michel? The interval before Jean started to inquire after her? The truth of any expressions have been rendered so doubtful, the linguistic links have become so few and tenuous, that her reaction virtually negates any impact that Monique's revelation might have had; it falls oddly flat. What one is left with is Véra's sense of loss and disappointment, without a clear sense of what has occasioned it.

The scene's final revelation is even more abrupt. Monique announces that Bernard Fontaine died in a car crash the day before yesterday. This seemingly casual announcement is introduced with no preparation, and Véra's hesitant admission that she found him attractive, in itself, would make this revelation fall as flat as the previous one. This time, however, both the revelation and the reaction are underscored by the sounds of the Turbulence, lending the interchange a tension and significance completely lacking in the words. Duras uses the side text to heighten the expressive quality, while keeping the main text flat, almost deadpan. Another enigma is added to the tale, that of "Bernard Fontaine," who appears to be linked to the story only by the fact that Véra found him attractive. Another name, linked to another nebulous desire.

As we have moved from the play's first reference to Véra Baxter to the end of the first scene with her, the number of verified assertions made about her have been few, and her presence has done little, if anything, to clear up the enigmas surrounding her. She has remained distant, and Duras has run the risk that such sustained vagueness and distance will bore her audience. Unrelieved Otherness may be a fascinating intellectual concept, but it does minimize the possibility of active discourse. Johnson's (1987, 43-46) intriguing actantial models for the action of this play put Monique in the role of Véra's opponent, and that is no doubt the most appropriate function among the limited range of functions offered by actantial analysis. It is important to note, however, how few and attenuated the expressions of opposition are in the main text. Linguistic oppositions are almost non-existent in their scene. Duras gives Monique the actantial function of the opponent in the level of plot, but does not give her the language of opposition that would give the function theatrical presence.

Luckily, the next scene moves us closer to Véra, and brings stronger manifestative qualities to the surface. We see her in a telephone conversation with her husband, a figure who, in contrast with Véra, has been strongly characterized. This scene has been built up to ever since the first moments of the play, when the Bartender talked to Jean, and has been reiterated in each succeeding scene. The importance of the scene was further developed when Véra told Monique that she was going to talk on the phone to Jean about Michel, making us to expect a major revelation that will have an effect on the development of the plot. It will be, after all, a truth that will break through the system of lies, we assume. It is, to use the old-fashioned language of the well-made play for a moment, an obligatory scene, and Duras handles it deftly. She keeps the more active and more strongly defined character offstage, reducing him to a voice, while keeping the enigmatic, even indeterminate, character before our eyes. We hang on her every movement and reaction as she talks with him.

The scene begins with a conversation about The Colonnades, rather than a revelation about Michel. Duras establishes suspense by not broaching that subject immediately, but by beginning with the pretense for the call. Yet, underneath this pretense, Duras establishes states of affairs that go beyond the discussion of a summer rental, and communicate a crisis within the marriage itself. The sense of acute dislocation begins with the way the conversation itself is heard by us. Jean's voice, the side text tells us, is amplified but slightly muffled, giving us a non-realistic presentation of the scene. The main text seems realistic enough at first, but heightens the tension and manifestative qualities conveying Véra's desperation by giving her lines that project a series of states of affairs of great anguish. When Jean asks her where she is, she replies "Je ne sais plus" (56) [I don't know any more (30)]. On a realistic level, this assertion makes little sense. We know where Véra is, and the context of the entire scene shows that she knows as well. It is, rather, an expression of her deep sense of dislocation; she responds to his question about physical location with an answer about her spiritual state.

Even when their expressions relate directly to the house, they are inflated beyond the level of language needed to refer to it. "Il aurait peut-être fallu changer d'endroits...de tout...de tout..." (57) [Maybe we should have changed towns...everything... everything (30)], says Véra. The idea of looking for another place to vacation in becomes expanded into the largest possible notion of change. The repeated "tout," with ellipsis marks after it, gives those words an added weight. We've yet to learn what is occasioning this crisis, but our sense of it is growing more acute. It builds as Jean replies with a bland "On a essayé aussi" (57) [We've tried that too (30)]. The fatuousness of the reply is clear; one cannot possibly have tried everything as well. His assertion conveys the impossibility of doing anything more than they have done already; an assertion that provokes a cry from Véra. Cody (1988, 21) has rightly remarked of Duras's plays in general that "conflict never emerges in the histrionic sense," but this scene is a rare exception. It has a traditional climactic form, as the protagonist grows more anxious, and peaks with a revelation.

But the structure, however traditional, advances through far more ambiguous assertions and elliptical constructions than the confrontation between husband and wife in *A Doll House*; in fact, it is impossible to tell just what is motivating the climax. Rather than being clearly articulated on the level of plot or intellectual argument, the scene reaches its moment of greatest intensity through the development of the theme of lies. When Véra insists that she does nothing but lie, her husband counters with "Il ny a que toi qui dise la vérité" (59) [You're the only one who tells the truth (31)]. The truth of Véra's statement is impossible to ascertain. If she does in fact, lie all the time, than this assertion is in itself a lie; an example of the famous antinomy of the liar. It becomes more troubling, though, because it is placed in the context of a scene in which Véra does not say anything that is demonstrably false; in fact, her statements about the house and Monique seem true. The best conclusion is that it is rhetorically in keeping with earlier statements of hers in the scene as hyperbole born of desperation; she is experiencing her own tendency toward untruth, for whatever reasons, intensely. Jean's response tries to efface her anxiety, to define Véra as the sole locus of truth (Véra/vérité). The clash between her intense, subjective experience of falsehood and his assured imposition of an exalted purity on her leads to greater tension: the Turbulence rises up, Véra screams, and announces "c'est fini" (59) [It's over (31)] repeatedly, ending with the accusation "tu le savais" (59) [You knew it (31)].

As audience, we see Jean's assertion and Véra's anguished revelation as related, if only by simple juxtaposition. But, since there are no linguistic links between the two statements, we are lead to search for unity within the extralinguistic situation. Either Jean's assertion directly elicits Véra's revelation, or the prelinguistic judgment to make this revelation has been made earlier and has continued, unspoken, throughout the scene to this point, where it suddenly intrudes, without any direct link to the preceding statement. Once again, Duras keeps her moment of revelation ambiguous: we are not sure what is over, or what he knew. Unlike Nora and Torvald, who analyze and counter each other's accusations with the skill of collegiate debaters, Véra and Jean do not sustain the moments that have the potential to develop into disputes. No sooner does Véra make her accusation than she leaves the subject; Jean responds with an expression that is linguistically linked to hers, but which is so general as to offer us no solutions to any of the enigmas: "Je ne sais plus rien" (60) [I don't know anything any more (31)]. This line echoes Michel's much earlier admission that he has mysteriously lost Véra, and links to all of the play's enunciations of the theme of Véra as unknowable, but these links are thematic and general, not the specific links of active discourse. As a result, Véra's moment of accusation is brief, unsustained, and quickly transforms itself into despair. She will go off with Michel, or perhaps commit suicide. Her accusation becomes a self-accusation; "Je n'aime plus rien. Plus personne" (61) [I don't love anybody any more (31)].

The development of Véra takes on a further interior dimension with this admission. The social nullity that kept her from being the object of assertions in the earlier scenes, and the evasiveness that kept her from revealing herself to Monique, here finds its inner equivalent in an absence of desire. Véra is defined by negation, by absence, even within herself. This emphasis on absence is a common aspect of Duras's protagonists (Cody 1988, 20), but the admission becomes particularly problematic here, for by this time, after repeated assertions that the protagonist lies, the truth of any expression of hers must be questioned. So even an expression of absent desire is qualified by an overall context of dubiousness. Véra is absent even in her most personal assertion of absence.

This absence is qualified somewhat in the final scene, as the Customer, now renamed "the Stranger," re-enters for a meeting with Véra. In this metadrama, it is the spectator alone who can help the protagonist constitute a narrative about herself. Not that this narrative is free from ambiguities: one moment, it is not clear when Véra learned about her husband's role in arranging her affair with Michel, nor when the affair took place, nor whether she was unfaithful to her husband with Michel, Bernard Fontaine, or some anonymous man in a café. Although on the surface *Véra Baxter* has many of the attributes of realism, the work is shot through with contradictory states of affairs. The moment and occasion of infidelity remain unknown; the feelings of desire and betrayal cannot be relegated to a single, unquestionable origin. The play takes the plot and character conventions of the domestic drama--infidelity and family finances, the philandering husband and the tempted wife, the gigolo who falls in love and the scheming mistress--but cuts them loose from the illusion that they exist in a world like ours. In *Véra Baxter*, the final meeting is between a character who exists totally within the presented world, and another character who exists both within it as a character and outside of it as an audience member. Here, bourgeois realistic drama becomes metadrama.

For the desire of the Stranger, begun with hearing the name "Véra Baxter" in the bar, and the Véra's desire, begin to interact. As she tells her story, the Stranger begins to respond to it, moving from curiosity to empathic involvement:

C'est curieux...cette douleur...quand vous avez raconté...*là*[side text] Comme si je venais de vous perdre à mon tour.(97)	It's strange...that pain..when you were talking..."there." [side text] As if I too had just lost you.(39)

The tempo is slow, the rhythms are hesitant, the intense indications of emotion heard in the previous scene are absent. The verbs are in the past, in the tense of fictional narration. The language is only active to the extent that the Stranger is trying to elicit Véra's narrative; her narrative, on the other hand, seems to have no motivation to shape or change him. This dynamic moves the play in the direction of being less a play about theatre, and more a play about narrative, a tendency that has become more pronounced in her later work, such as *The Malady of Death*, in which she combines a performer speaking from memory with one who is reading from the text (Willis 1989, 110-111). The impulse to pairing is frustrated in the interest of an exploration of the dynamics of textuality; actors become readers. This tendency is less pronounced in *Véra Baxter*, but it is there nonetheless, and accounts in part for the less active quality of discourse here.

The Stranger not only elicits Véra's story from herself, but adds to it. The climactic revelation about Véra in this scene comes from him, as he adds a mythic dimension to her story. The attraction of her name, he explains, comes from the fact that he remembered it. It was the name of a woman during the Crusades who began talking to the creatures and forces of nature in her husband's absence. We are never told how he knows this; it is not realistically justified. But it makes the story of the contemporary Véra a remembrance, not having its point of origin in the bar, but an incident centuries ago. The desire of the Stranger was provoked by an impossible recollection. "Duras' texts always remember" (Willis 1989, 110), and the Stranger's memory supplements Véra's own, and restores an earlier, forgotten Véra into the play.

With the two Véras restored to each other, a more reciprocal interchange between the two onstage characters becomes possible. Véra admits, as she did in the previous scene, to her lack of desire, but the Stranger, rather than evading this assertion, answers it, forging a linguistic link between her despair and his language. He points out that she has wanted to die, and that in itself is a desire. She, then, turns, and, for the first time, tries to forge a connection between her desires and his:

| Dès que vous avez parlé (*arrêt*) j'ai deviné (*arrêt*) que vous aussi...une fois...vous aviez voulu mourir. (107) | As soon as you began talking (*stop*) I guessed that you too... at one point...had wanted to die (41) |

The loneliness that has been connected with Véra (her isolation in the house, her repeated anxiety that no one could hear you scream there) is bridged by the recognition of a similar desire in another character. The common experience of despair bridges the gap between character and viewer, man and woman. What Véra has intuited is not so much the Stranger's story, but the trace of a past experience manifesting itself in his voice. He assents to that as a "identité possible" (107) [possible identity (41)], and the Turbulence, repeatedly connected with estrangement, slowly dies away.

This bond established, Véra can leave the Colonnades, in the company of the Stranger. Conversation continues, even after they have passed out of sight. Duras has charted a movement from alienation to conversation, from estrangement to the possibility of shared experience. The restoration of the long-dead Véra to her present counterpart, by the shores of the Atlantic, changing the tone from one of mourning to a re-engagement with life, echoes the late romances of Shakespeare, with their grieving fathers and miraculously reappearing wives and daughters. But Duras' voice is more muted than Shakespeare's; perhaps even too muted for the stage. While Shakespeare works to strengthen the illusion of his characters' full presence before the audience, Duras renders them insubstantial, to the extent that they finally exit "insensiblement" (110) [imperceptibly (41)]. Their emotional lives manifest themselves briefly, and then often in muffled and ambiguous forms. Even language can be reduced to the level of an indication. *Véra Baxter* exists at a certain boundary, where revelation is desired, and yet only briefly granted. It is a purgatory in which the characters are kept distant from each other, and from us.

STRANGE MUSIC:
"THE HUNTING PARTY"

From *Inadmissible Evidence* to *Véra Baxter*, we have seen dramatic conflict and confrontation grow more attenuated. But Duras' artful proliferation of enigmas and sexual intrigue makes *Véra Baxter* seem a labyrinth of plot complication compared to Thomas Bernhard's austerely fashioned *The Hunting Party* [*Die Jagdgesellschaft*]. A synopsis of the play is quickly provided; it is the simplest of simple plots. The General, who suffers from cataracts, as well as some unspecified illness that may be fatal, may or may not know that the forest of his estate is completely infested with bark beetles. When the General challenges the Writer, who is a friend of the General's Wife, to fashion a comedy about him and his guests, the Writer replies with a caustic and nihilistic description of life. The General shoots himself.

At the climax of this full-length play, the protagonist elaborates a general situation that would not seem to imperil anyone directly, and thus hastens what would seem to be the inevitable demise of another character. Although *The Hunting Party* contains moments of tension and even antagonism among its various characters, it does not sustain any of them. The closest thing to a superobjective is the Writer's desire to reveal the infestation of the forest to the General. Yet, it is not altogether clear that the General is ignorant of the fact. His ignorance is simply asserted by his Wife, who wishes to protect him from the fact:

Ich habe eine Mauer des Schweigens um ihn aufgerichtet er darf von Börkenkäfer nichts wissen (Bernhard 1974, 42).	I have erected a wall of silence around him he must not know anything about the bark beetle [trans. RFG]

Yet there are indications that the forest is already a source of anxiety for the General, suggesting that he may know something about the bark beetles. He finds the woodcutters threatening, and went out in the woods one day with a power saw, only to cut himself with it. Besides, even if the General were ignorant of the bark beetle, the Writer's climactic speech at the party scarcely mentions it at all. The General's Wife, the only character who hears of the Writer's objective, ignores his assertions for some time, and talks of other things, only to gradually assent to everything he says. The tension between the two characters quickly vanishes in the course of the first act. In the second act, there is no tension between them, the plot does not advance, and the primary piece of stage business is a lengthy game of cards. In the third act, no one tries to prevent or challenge the Writer's revelations. It is the General who challenges the Writer to speak, accepts his statements without protest, leaves the room in silence, and shoots himself.

The lack of conflict in the sequence of events is reflected in the lack of conflicting linguistic contexts in the main text. Bernhard does not present the conflict of semantic contexts in the form of a dispute. Instead, he juxtaposes two ongoing monologues, thus showing that the two speakers are incapable of conducting a conversation, dispute, dialogue or situational discourse with each other. The psychological distance is manifested by this lack of conflict is far greater than the distance manifested by stichomythia. In stichomythia, the characters exhibit opposing viewpoints on a common topic. Here, the characters refuse to address a common topic. The speeches do not develop in dialectical progression, but develop unmodified by each other. For example, when the Writer suddenly reveals:

Ich weiß jetzt alles über den Börkenkäfer	I now know everything about the bark beetle

alles gnädige Frau Und über die Augenkrankheit welche als Graue Star bezeichnet wird (21)	everything dear lady and about the eye disease which is called cataract

the General's Wife continues to talk about nightfall on the estate and the difficulties of heating the hunting lodge. Only after eight speeches maintain this tension between the Writer and the General's Wife does she admit, albeit indirectly, that the Writer's assertions have been correct. The dramatic tension here is not manifested through overt challenge, but through mutual withdrawal into personal realms of repeated monologic assertion. Dialectical development is impossible, and the General's Wife at length submits to her adversary's assertions, rather than attempting to modify them. Only two linguistic options present themselves to the characters in *The Hunting Party* and these options correspond to two fundamental social roles. Either one submits to the other's monologic frame of values completely, becoming the slave, or one withdraws into a completely separate monologic context that cannot enter into dialogue with any other speaker and tries to coerce the other characters into total submission. Since the alternatives are capitulation, reassertion, or withdrawal, productive opposition is an impossibility here. This dynamic appears in many of Bernhard's plays, which are dominated by characters who monomaniacally force their wills on those around them, including, among others, the Good Woman in *A Party for Boris* [*Ein Fest für Boris*], the Doctor in *The Ignoramus and the Madman* [*Der Ignorant und der Wahnsinnige*], Caribaldi in *The Force of Habit* [*Die Macht der Gewohnheit*], and the title characters in *Immanuel Kant* and *The Theatremaker* [*Der Theatermacher*]. For all these characters (and many others in Bernhard's *oeuvre*), language exists only as a means of exercising power.

In *The Hunting Party*, the Writer comes to project his deeply pessimistic view of existence so vividly that it envelops the entire presented world, both causing the General's suicide and elucidating the view of life that underlies the action. In contrast to Maitland, the Writer does not dominate the play through his emotional intensity and psychological complexity, but through the clarity and eloquence of his vision. Osborne establishes the extremes of his *Inadmissible*

Evidence's emotional range through the extremes of emotion manifested by his protagonist. Bernhard establishes his protagonist as the most intense and intellectually sophisticated proponent of a philosophical viewpoint, and subordinates the perceptions of all the other characters to that.

Bernhard is careful not to let any of the other characters challenge the Writer's domination of the play: two of them, Anna and the Prince, never speak; the Princess utters a single word; the ministers speak their few lines in unison; and Asamer's few lines neither establish character nor contribute to the play's dominant themes. Only the General and his Wife speak at length, and their presences are clearly secondary to the Writer's. The General's Wife is onstage for the entire play, but she does not talk about herself, but about housekeeping, cards, her husband, and her guests.

The General is the most divided and, therefore, most potentially interesting character. He is caught between his knowledge of death, represented by the motif of the Battle of Stalingrad, and his own flight from death, represented by the motif of his own flight from his would-be killers in the forest. Bernhard, however, carefully prevents him from dominating the action. He keeps the General offstage for most of the first scene and none of the second, and his memories of Stalingrad, his feelings about his own illness, his knowledge (if any) of the bark beetle, and the reasons for his suicide are not projected through his own expressions. When he is onstage, he mostly talks about the Writer.

It is only in the third scene that the spectator is able to observe him at length, and, even then, his mental processes are obscure. None of his inner divisions are manifested in his speeches. He never tries to prevent the Writer's revelation, nor does he utter a single word in response to it. He lapses into a silence that is only defined by his offstage suicide. Because of the lack of verbal definition, even his single defining action remains difficult to interpret. Is it stoic acceptance or abysmal despair? Tragic insight or further retreat? The movement from self-delusion to suicide is not dramatized so the spectator can experience a series of psychic states along with the General. Rather, his suicide is viewed completely externally, as a static emblem of death's omnipotence. A pistol shot is heard, and the Prince opens the door; there lies the General, dead. The corpse lies in what amounts to an inner stage, a tableau that can be observed, but not entered into.

The most important aspects of the General are projected through the descriptions of others, rather than his own speech. Since the assertions about the General are never directly confirmed by the actions and expressions of the General, the character never completely coalesces. We do not feel that we know him with the same certainty that we know Maitland or Shakespeare. As a result, the Writer, who is the simpler, less divided character, remains the most fully developed presence in the play.

The Writer's position is further also strengthened because Bernhard always allows the states of affairs that the Writer projects to stand, without challenge from the other characters. The General's Wife can only temporarily ignore, not challenge, his revelation that he knows about the General's cataracts and the forest's infestation. She does not attempt to refute his philosophy of death, and the General, from the beginning of the Writer's climactic speech, lapses into silence. None of the Writer's assertions lead to disputes; the power of his language goes unchecked.

In the first scene, the Writer expresses states of affairs that were supposedly secret. In the second, he articulates a philosophical framework for the play. In the last scene, he becomes nothing less than the presenter of *The Hunting Party* itself, as he describes the onstage situation as a situation to be presented in a play of his own devising:

Eine Komödie stellen sich vor in welcher ein General eine Hauptrolle spielt und dieser General hat eine Todeskrankheit in Stalingrad haben sie ihm den linken Arm abgerissen Und eines Tages geht er in den Wald und verletzt sich mit der Motorsäge am Bein (104).	Imagine a comedy in which a general plays a leading role and this general has a fatal disease in Stalingrad they ripped off his left arm And one day he goes into the woods And injures himself in the leg with a power saw

In this speech, the Writer projects a series of statements about a play that coincides with the one that Bernhard has written. In so doing, the

Writer momentarily appears to transcend his world and control it. His projected statements fuse completely with Bernhard's presentation of a fictive world, and the world established by the presented text and the verbal world established by a character within that text become virtually indistinguishable. The Writer's privileged position limits the possibilities for dispute or dialogue, since his speeches seemingly determine both the philosophical standpoint of the play and its action. His monologic context is never threatened by the objections of other characters, by events within the presented world, or by his own self-criticism. He is as stationary as Maitland is vacillating.

Because the extralinguistic situation never modifies the expressions of the protagonist, he remains a static figure. He elaborates on the play's intellectual argument at some length, but neither the emotional state of the protagonist nor the attitudes of the other characters seem significantly altered as a result. The static presented world is virtually indistinguishable from the static world view presented by the protagonist. This view of life is essentially monadic; it can be restated an infinite number of times, but cannot alter. Both the play and its protagonist assert the omnipotence and omnipresence of death--all existence is under its sway. The Writer's exclusive interest in death coincides with *The Hunting Party*'s, an obsessional theme is reiterated by an obsessive character within a presented world that is itself characterized by reiteration and obsessive repetition. Thus, conflict and dialectical interaction are replaced by repetition. Instead of a continuous development of varied psychic states through character interaction, the spectator witnesses the intensification of a thesis.

Bernhard softens the contrasts between his speakers' individual verbal styles not only to preserve the coherence of the whole, but to structure a world completely under the control of the states of affairs projected by the Writer. As Mann has pointed out, lyric drama is distinguished by the way the presentative quality of the text makes itself felt through "a pattern of limited differentiation" (1988, 22) among the speeches in the main text, which keeps us aware of a single origin to all speeches, overriding our sense of highly individualized characters. For, the greater the similarity of vocabulary and word order in the various speeches of the main text, the more the spectator is made aware of the presence of a single presenter behind all of those speeches. The illusion of autonomous character is diminished or even destroyed, and a single, lyric, presentative voice emerges more strongly from the playtext.

The Hunting Party

Bernhard's homogeneous speech contrasts strongly with the desire for linguistic variety in the plays of Bond and Osborne, and brings him closer to Duras. Unlike Bond's landowners and peasants all of Bernhard's characters speak in the same manner, use similar images, and share a common vocabulary. Bernhard deals with a very limited range of characters who either share a common range of obsessions or fall silent.

Although obsessions are often rich in manifestative qualities (Harpagon, Hilde Wangel, and Reverend Davidson being only three notable examples of the theatrically obsessed), Bernhard uses his characters' psychological fixations to limit their emotional responses. In the second scene, the Writer continues to play cards with the General's Wife throughout his lengthy, nihilistic harangue. Despite the intensity of his grim philosophical speculations, he never becomes so emotionally involved with them that he loses track of the game. Habit overrides intensity. Indeed, the greatest manifestation of intense interest in *The Hunting Party* emerges from habitual manifestations of obsessions that are trivial in their object. The card game is one such obsession:

>   noch noch noch   on on on
>   wir spielen   we play
>   wir spielen weiter   we keep playing
>   wir spielen als ob wir   we play as if we
>   verrückt werden wollten   wanted to go crazy
>   (18).

The card game imposes an outer limit on the intensity of the manifestative qualities in the second scene. No action can exceed the card game in intensity, since it takes precedence over everything else:

>   Wir bezichtigen die Individuen   We accuse the individ-
>   der Charakterschwäche   ual
>   gnädige Frau   of character weaknesses
>   und wir berufen uns gleich-   dear lady
>   zeitig   and we simultaneously
>   auf die Ungerechtigkeit   note
>   wie auf das Recht   the injustice
>   aber das Leben   as well as the justice

oder besser die Existenz	but life
(*ruft aus*)	or better existence
Gewonnen	(*calls out*)
(*wirft die Karten auf den Tisch*)	I've won
ist ein Alptraum (71).	(*throws his cards on the table*)
	is a nightmare

The Writer's central tenet, that existence is a nightmare, is obviously not demanding his undivided attention, since he interrupts his observations right before their completion to announce that he has won the hand. Stage business provides the strongest indications of emotion here, qualifying the emotional intensity implied by some of the speeches in the main text.

This subordination of an intensely pessimistic philosophical tirade to the demands of a card game is a striking example of Bernhard's talent for ironic stage comedy. Rather than letting this macabre vision completely dominate the stage as it is articulated, Bernhard puts it into perspective by interrupting it with a card game. Morbid pessimism and frivolous entertainment co-exist so comfortably in the mind of the Writer that the two obsessions are reduced to a common level. Eisner, who is virtually alone among critics in appreciating the tremendous wit of Bernhard's plays, is right in pointing out that the use of such techniques "puts into question, of not completely destroys, the ostensibly tragic nature of this play" (1987, 110). Bernhard establishes a comic irony by undercutting our expectation that deep philosophical pessimism necessarily goes hand in hand with deep emotional intensity.

Even the opposition between the General and the Writer avoids disputation. Although the General's Wife describes her husband's relationship to the Writer in terms that would make us expect the fiercest antagonism onstage:

Er haßt Sie	He hates you
aber nicht so tief	but not as deeply
Wie Sie ihn hassen (60)	As you hate him

but their scenes together avoid direct confrontation. In the first scene, the General holds forth that the Writer's contradictory theatre piece, which runs the gamut from tragedy to operetta, but he never develops it in the form of a dispute, defining he and the Writer against each other. Nor does the Writer respond. The General's tone is scornful, but his speech remains formal, and largely in the third person. In the last scene, both the General and the Writer have long speeches, but they do not alternate; once the writer begins to speak, the General falls silent for the remainder of the play. In his climactic speech, the Writer does not set up verbal oppositions or antitheses between the General and himself; rather, the speech most frequently makes use of the first person plural pronoun, projecting a universal state of affairs. As his speech builds, he abandons his own voice entirely, and reads a passage from Lermontov's *A Hero of Our Time*, manifesting a greater impersonality and remove by quoting a lengthy passage that develops the themes of the play through a different voice, in the words of a character who exists within a completely different presented world.

Indeed, the hatred that the General's Wife speaks of never clearly manifests itself in the Writer's speeches; it seems to be Bernhard's heterodox strategy throughout this play to have characters make assertions about other characters that we do not see express themselves in action. More than once, the Writer comments approvingly on the General's writing, and particularly on his ability to write about death, the Writer's favorite subject. "Er hat einen Blick für die Toten" (110) [He has an eye for the dead], he comments approvingly. In a world in which all difference is continually eroded by the omnipotence of mortality, sustained opposition crumbles. The inability to sustain differentiation in a monadic universe leads to the inability to sustain dramatic conflict.

The lack of strong manifestative qualities throughout is of a piece with Bernhard's general lack of interest in characterization for its own sake here. It is not surprising that a playwright who has little interest in imbuing his characters with deep emotions would only sketch out the relationship between his characters schematically. The Prince, Princess, and Ministers are only minimally established, and then only in relationship to the General, and those relationships are established by the General's Wife in her speeches, rather than by their own dramatic actions or self-characterizations. Similarly, the relationship between the General and his Wife is less than vivid. Gampers (1977, 129) has suggested that the marriage is permeated with scorn and intense loathing, but he seems to be relying on the generalization that all Bernhardian couples, from the legless benefactress and her idiot husband in *A Party for Boris*, to the reclusive hearing specialist and his rifle-toting wife in *The Lime Works* [*Das Kalkwerk*], succeed in making Strindberg's *The Dance of Death* look like a celebration of married life. Actually, the relationship between the General and his spouse is difficult to define. The Wife neither defends her husband against the Writer, nor does she revel in his illness. Her characterization is subordinated to the thematic concerns of the play, which do not include domestic relationships. Although she is a major character, one searches in vain for her superobjective; indeed, it is difficult to establish any clear objectives for her behavior in the final scene. Written to fulfill the exigencies of each scene, she is clearly just another of the marionettes mentioned in Bernhard's epigraph to the play (a quotation from Kleist's "On the Marionette Theatre"), and our tendency to regard her as an autonomously existing agent within the presented world is undercut.

Stressing general truths over specific situations, minimizing conflict in both the linguistic and extralinguistic situations, and favoring description over action, Bernhard allows only a rigorously delimited range of expressive qualities to emerge. As a result, *The Hunting Party* runs the risk of exhausting its expressive qualities long before the curtain falls. Drama is present in the unfolding of a situation, but there is little to unfold in this play after the initial scene, and much of the material is simply repeated. There are only two points at which the extralinguistic situation is altered by the Writer's speeches: (1) when the General's Wife admits that both her husband and the forest are incurably diseased; and (2) when the General shoots himself. The vast majority of the speeches do not alter the extralinguistic context, and, as a result, the speeches develop their topics through the elaboration of themes and motifs, as might be seen in a lyric poem, instead of altering, and being altered by, the entire situation.

A note by Bernhard, appended to the printed version of *The Hunting Party*, further demonstrates this dramatist's lack of interest in traditional Western dramatic form: "Das Stück ist im drei Sätzen geschrieben, der letze Satz ist der 'langsame Satz'" (112) [The piece is written in three movements, the last movement is the "slow movement"]. Claus Peymann, who has directed the premieres of most of Bernhard's plays, said that most of Bernhard's comments to him about the plays used the vocabulary of music (1985, 191). Each scene is an expression, a lyric action that develops a constellation of images. Chambers (1976, 3) has suggested that the structures of Bernhard's plays are more akin to musical structures than conventionally dramatic structures, and Jurgensen (1981) has articulated a musical aesthetic at work in Bernhard's writing. Although analogies between music and literature are often fanciful and misleading, it is true that Bernhard's plays exhibit a greater fascination than usual with formal qualities of stage speech, such as repetition and aural patterning, than with the usual dramatic qualities of plot and character.

By far the most striking and idiosyncratic element in the main text of *The Hunting Party* is the absence of punctuation, a stylistic device that, I would argue, indicates a great deal about Bernhard's musical approach to dramatic speech. Punctuation is usually an important aid for both actors and silent readers of the main text, indicating much about the emotional tone of the speech. Both *Inadmissible Evidence* and *Bingo* use punctuation to stress certain words, suggest word groupings and pauses, and indicate the manner of delivery. Bond suggests Shakespeare's emotional exhaustion and the slowness with which his speeches are to be delivered by setting off short phrases and even individual words with periods. *Inadmissible Evidence* is particularly rich in its number and variety of punctuation marks, indicating the rapid shifts in the protagonist's mood and his continually changing mind:

> But that's well, I do drink a lot. Quite a lot? Oh,
> anyway, I'm what you'd call a serious drinker. That's
> to say, I just don't mess about once I get going--when
> I do. When I do? I nearly always do. (Osborne 1965, 14)

Rearranging Osborne's words in Bernhard's unpunctuated style, one immediately realizes the limitations imposed on the main text by Bernhard's choice. There are certain effects that Osborne can achieve that Bernhard must forego:

> But that's well
> I do drink quite a lot
> quite a lot
> oh anyway
> I'm what you'd call

> a serious drinker
> that's to say
> I just don't mess about
> once I get going
> when I do
> when I do
> I nearly always do

"Well" becomes ambiguous in this new setting; it is no longer clear whether it is synonymous with "fine" or a mere place-filler. The third line registers as a simple repetition, instead of a question, as does the penultimate line. The self-questioning qualities of the speech, which reveal Maitland's mental agility, agitation, and self-critical faculties, are lost in this Bernhardian version, which becomes less energetic and more brooding. The brooding quality is a function of the speeches' slower pace. Without punctuation, a clear sense of subordination is lost; every word appears to be of equal weight. In Osborne's speech, there is a clear sense of subordination. Phrases such as "Oh, anyway" and "That's to say" are set off by commas from the main clauses of the sentences in which they appear. They are clearly less important, and can be spoken with less emphasis. Bernhard's omission of punctuation lessens the differences of weight carried by each word in the main text, and removes both colloquial and conversational qualities from his plays. His speeches almost demand to be intoned, rather than spoken.

The highly formal qualities of Bernhard's main text are further illuminated by comparison to Osborne's speech. The German equivalents of "mess about" and "get going" are not to be found nearly so frequently in *The Hunting Party*. Questions, so numerous in *Inadmissible Evidence*, are absent. Bernhard's characters only express themselves in declarative and imperative statements, and self-interrogation is an experience foreign to Bernhard's assertive egoists. In short, few of the devices that Osborne uses to infuse his main text with strong emotional energy can be found in *The Hunting Party*. Colloquialisms, interjections, questions, exclamations and individually characterized speech are either omitted or severely limited.

At first, Bernhard's austere style might seem to render *The Hunting Party* unsuitable for theatrical production. Since the text minimizes manifestative qualities, and works to lessen the differences among them, theatrical representation would certainly add qualities that

Bernhard has taken pains to avoid. It might seem that the actor would have to combat his/her innate tendency to add color and expressiveness to his speeches, the director and designer would have to avoid making strong visual statements, and still the production would inevitably be more expressive than the text as Bernhard has presented it on the page. Bernhard performed, it might seem at first, is Bernhard betrayed.

Yet that conclusion is incorrect. Bernhard was eager to have his plays produced. He accepted commissions from the Salzburg Festival and wrote more than one role as a showpiece for the talents of a particular performer. His theatrical work has been frequently performed, and few playwrights of the 70s and 80s can match the fluency and consistency of his dramatic output. Bernhard's plays develop a theatrical aesthetic that is highly individual and expresses a *Weltanschauung* that is presented with almost obsessive consistency not only through his plays, but his novels, short fiction and autobiographical volumes as well.

His work is dominated by an acute awareness of human finitude. Our plans are always opposed by reality, which frustrates them and keeps them incomplete. The self wills that the world submit to its act of will, but the world is always stronger than the self. There are many ill-fated projects in Bernhard's works: Caribaldi in *The Force of Habit* to force a note-perfect rendition of Schubert's *Trout Quintet* from a circus troupe; Konrad in *The Lime Works* remains incapable of completing his treatise on hearing; the title character in *Minetti* will never return to the stage as King Lear; and the Blind Man in *The Ignoramus and the Madman* will never be able to perform a successful autopsy. *The Hunting Party* begins with the description of an uncompleted action. The Writer explains that he stayed awake throughout the night, trying to formulate an aphorism that he could never successfully complete. While he was trying to compose it, he kept opening and closing the window--closing it because he was cold, opening it "weil ich den Wahnsinn geschlossener Fenster/nicht beherrschte" (12) [because I could not control/the insanity of a closed window]. Both a closed window and an open window are unendurable, and he is driven to both perpetual movement and perpetual frustration. The problem of the window is, for Bernhard, a paradigm for the futility of all human endeavors. Art, science, politics, philosophy and human relationships are all doomed to endless incompleteness, and, hence, frustration. These fated obsessions are no simple labors of love; Bernhard's characters are as inclined to despise their projects as draw sustenance from them. The Writer and the General's Wife hate the card game they play so madly, and Caribaldi aptly summarizes the Bernhardian view of life and art:

> Wir wollen das Leben nicht
> aber es muß gelebt werden
> [...]
> Wir hassen den Forellen-
>   quintett
> aber es muß gespielt werden
> (Bernhard 1975, 123)

> We do not want life
> but it must be lived
> [...]
> We hate
> the Trout Quintet
> but it must be played

As a result of this bondage, Bernhard's artists come to hate their art, and hate above all the artistic tradition that enslaves them. In his most extended dramatic exploration of the artistic psyche, *Die Berühmten* [*The Celebrities*], an operatic soprano accidentally decapitates an effigy of Lotte Lehmann with a champaigne bottle, and her fellow artists suddenly erupt in an orgy of destruction, fiendishly devising macabre ends for effigies of Arturo Toscanini, Richard Tauber, Max Reinhardt, and other celebrated predecessors.

All artistic activity is wedded to hatred and pain. The General's writing forces him to recount the horrors of the Battle of Stalingrad, which dominates his memoirs as it dominates his memory. He disgusts his wife with his descriptions of the frozen, snow-covered corpses. Art is inescapable and authoritarian; it attempts to force an arbitrary and personal order onto reality. The brutality of all Bernhard's artists and monologists embodies the brutality in all attempts to create order, whether political, domestic, philosophical, scientific, or aesthetic. Like the *Trout Quintet*, which is hated but must be played, order is loathsome but must be imposed.

All human attempts to impose a system are ultimately ludicrous, Procrustean, and doomed to failure, because of humanity's radical imperfection. Both our perceptions and our expressions of those perceptions are flawed. The gap between what we perceive and what actually exists may be so great that we can never know what really exists. A number of Bernhard's characters suffer from diseases of the eye, including the Father in *The Ignoramus and the Madman*, Immanuel Kant, the Princess, and the General. We are told that the

Princess is so near-sighted that she is almost blind. Yet, when the characters stand at the window, looking out at the winter night, she utters her only word in the entire play, "Schön" (106) [Lovely]. This single word, set off by pauses, is the only appreciation of beauty in this otherwise grisly work. Its positive import, however, is rendered problematic, even ludicrous, by the flawed perception of the speaker. Does she see anything, or is she merely parroting social convention? If she sees anything, we do not know what she actually sees, or if her vision bears any resemblance to what the other characters perceive. Furthermore, we do not know what she means by her expression. What *is* "schön"? What idea of beauty does the Princess have? The word is isolated from any context that might render it intelligible. Here, first perception, then language, fail. For Bernhard, our expressions fail to convey our intentionality:

| Das Beschriebene meine Herrn ist etwas Anderes wie ja schon das Beobachtete etwas Anderes ist Alles ist anders (105) | The description gentlemen is something else just as the observation is already something else It is all something else |

Each character is imprisoned, and cannot either perceive his/her situation clearly, or communicate it clearly to anyone in the adjacent cells. In fact, it is never clear to them that there *is* an adjacent cell. The philosophical premises of the presented world are profoundly anti-theatrical in their implications, since not only is the gulf between each character unbridgeable, but the speeches are alienated from their underlying prelinguistic states as well. The language asks to be taken as an end in itself, since it is no longer a certain means of revealing psychic states. All action is doomed to frustration; no emotional states can be communicated.

Only death is certain. At the end of World War II, the General hid in the woods surrounding his hunting lodge to escape violent death. Thematically, this flight from death is linked to a flight from the spectacle of widespread death that he had witnessed at the Battle of Stalingrad. He has stayed in the forest, which is itself dying of disease, never allowing himself to fully realize that he carries his mortality within himself. Bernhard's figure of death never comes from outside the situation, like the Angel of Death or Maeterlinck's Intruder, but is rooted within the nature of every living creature. Bernhard's vision of mortality, in which death is a constituent of existence, rather than a simple negation of it, is reminiscent of the view articulated in Heidegger's *Being and Time* (Gross 1980, 365-66) The General's self-willed blindness to mortality is an unsuccessful attempt to hide from the images of Stalingrad that continue to haunt him. He has even sensed the imminent destruction of the forest; one day he set off into it with a power saw, and wounded himself while attempting to fell a tree. The awareness of death is a constant threat to the continuance of daily life. Card games, theatrical productions, writing, and, ironically, hunting, all seek to obscure the prospect of death.

Only the Writer is able to proclaim the omnipresence of death:

Wenn es etwas ist	If it is something
der Tod ist es	it is death
Wir hören eine Stimme	We hear a voice
(*Schüsse draußen*)	(*Shots outside*)
wir fragen	we ask
Der Tod ist es	It is death
Dieser schöne Mensch sagen wir	This beautiful person we say
Der Tod ist es	It is death
Dieses exakte Werk	This precise machine
Der Tod ist es (67-68).	It is death

He intones this litany of death to the General's Wife, who does not wish to speak or hear of death. He reads aloud from the writings of Lermontov, appreciating the cynical acceptance of death in *A Hero of Our Time*. He reveals to the General his impending death, and thus brings about the General's suicide. In this world of restlessness and frustrated order, the only stasis is that of death.

The theme of death is associated with motifs of cold and silence: Stalingrad was cold and silent; the Writer saw a woman killed by falling ice in Warsaw; the hunting lodge is difficult to heat; and the night of the General's suicide is cold and clear. Everything living and imperfect exists on an absolutely frozen foundation. The only successful actions destroy life; the trees are felled and the General shoots himself. All of the actions are played out against humanity's ultimate reduction to inert matter. "Jeder Gegenstand gnädige Frau," says the Writer, "ist der Tod" [Each circumstance dear lady is death] (69).

The austerity of Bernhard's style is at one with the austerity of his vision. Everything is a disguised form of death, about to collapse into the vacuum that it carries within itself. In the light of that truth, everything else becomes trivial; setting, personal emotion, characterization and plot complication dwindle into insignificance in the presence of death. *The Hunting Party*, like the Writer, proclaims death as the sole reality. Unlike Ibsen in *The Wild Duck*, Bernhard is not interested in presenting the varied and highly particularized strategies that unique individuals develop to protect themselves from varied and highly particularized threats. He is only interested in projecting a single, universal threat.

Certain expressive qualities, however, do arise from the main text, and Bernhard is very skillful in eliciting qualities from the contrast between words and silence. The silences in *The Hunting Party* are not active refusals to communicate, as in *Bingo*. Here, silence is the background for all expression, the stasis that enfolds all human actions, the quiet of death. The Writer links the motif of silence to those of coldness and death when she tells how he spent three days in Krakow without exchanging a single word in conversation. The characters assert themselves against the silence, which inevitably makes its presence felt. Silence surrounds our every statement, and even our most passionate assertions cannot extend themselves indefinitely.

Bernhard Dauenhauer, who has elaborated on Edmund Husserl's observations on silence in *The Phenomenology of Internal Time Consciousness*, has differentiated between several types of silence (Dauenhauer 1973, 9-27; 1976, 63-83). The silence that follows an expression is at first saturated with the sense of that preceding expression. As the silence lengthens, the saturation diminishes, though it never loses all traces of the preceding expression. Eventually, the silence begins to "open up" and anticipate the following expression. Every silence is initiated by the intention to complete the preceding expression, either because the speaker is satisfied with it or because s/he feels unable to improve upon it, and every silence opens up in anticipation of the new expression that will end it. The finished expression is never sufficient; something always remains to be said. The next expression will either add to the linguistic context, or reassert the preceding expression against the silence which has diminished its presence. The obsessive repetitions of *The Hunting Party* convey an intense sensation of the mortality of each expression that underlies the urge to repeat. It is not enough to assert one's context once; the silence eats away at it. The next moment it is necessary to assert it again:

Die Sprechenden hören	To hear the speaking
aber nicht sehen	but not see
Das Feuer im Ofen hören	To hear the fire in the
aber nichts sehen	stove
Das Feuer im Ofen hören	but see nothing
aber nichts sehen	To hear the fire in the
oder wenigstens nur so	stove
daß es nicht schmerzt (30).	but see nothing
	or at least only so much
	that it does not hurt

The intervening silence silences, implied in the text by the white space of page after every five or six syllables here, break the sentences into fragments. Each silence both gives a weight of the phrase that precedes it, and points up its limits. Dauenhauer has labeled this phenomenon "terminal silence" (1976: 76). Terminal silence emphasizes what has been uttered, since it allows the listener to ponder the expression in its entirety, after s/he has constituted the expression from the individual words. Dauenhauer describes the gravity given to an expression by terminal silence:

> This digesting, which adds nothing determinate to the expression *qua* expression, is the cut in the stream which allows a specific expression to achieve its existential weight. (1976, 76)

Terminal silence can be used by the dramatist as a foregrounding device, thereby allowing short or otherwise insignificant speeches to create a stronger effect than they would in an uninterrupted stream of expressions. No comment is subordinate or parenthetical; each has the force of a complete and independent expression.

Bernhard's speeches are often tightly constructed vessels on a sea of silence. The tightness is sometimes achieved through parallel constructions or repetitions. Or the words are arranged chiastically, creating a tension closed within elements of a terse speech:

Wir verachten	We despise
was wir hören	what we hear
Was wir sehen	What we see
verachten wir (70)	we despise

Or:

Ihm nicht	Him no
Nicht ihm (42).	Not him

Surrounded by silence, these are closed systems of verbal tension. The second half of each expression reverses the order of the first half, leading us back to the first word of the expression. This closure is the verbal equivalent of the Writer opening and closing his window in frustration. The frustrating circles that rule over Bernhard's characters find their linguistic expression in constructions such as these.

The combination of silence and repetition can give a ritual quality to stage speech: words and expressions are never casual or thrown away, but highly deliberate. Adding this to Bernhard's tendency not to sharply individualize his characters' speech, the main text takes on an impersonal, ritualized quality. The combination of silence, repetition, restricted vocabulary, and nearly equal emphasis on each element in an expression, as well as the severe limitation of manifestative qualities, gives *The Hunting Party* a ritualistic quality. In a ritual, the words are important in themselves, and the personal qualities of the speaker are essentially unimportant to them. All partcipants are depersonalized as they assume the roles that the ritual requires. The emphasis is not on the pathos of the sacrificial victim, but the impersonality of the action. It must be kept in mind, however, that the death of the General has none of the efficacy of a religious ritual, but is hot through with irony and sardonic humor. To the extent that *The Hunting Party* is a ritual, it is one that mocks itself.

Bernhard's characters exist less in opposition to each other than in opposition to death and silence. This playwright gives us a heightened awareness of the relationship between speech and silence, and uses it as a means of heightening our awareness of the inherent finitude of human existence. It is this revelation of spoken words, existing in conflict with the silence that surrounds them, that gives Bernhard's plays theatricality; only in performance can the interaction between words and silence fulfill the potential of the written text. The expressive qualities emerge from the main text, but they are only to a slight degree manifestations of the characters' psychic acts; these characters are highly generalized figures who serve the function of presenting the dramatist's images. In *Bingo*, we are affected both by Shakespeare's description of the bear-baiting and by his reaction to that event. In *The Hunting Party*, the narrated event dominates the manifestative qualities of the act of narration. The Writer and the General's Wife, two characters far removed from the horror, discuss the General's memories of Stalingrad. The vision projected by the characters provides us with a static object of contemplation, a self-contained presented universe that doubts whether we or the author can comprehend it. Such radical skepticism renders the creation of art absurd, and Bernhard's works question their own value with both bitter vindictiveness and trenchant wit.

The only positive image of human life in *The Hunting Party* is that of music. Classical music is played on the phonograph during two key sequences; in the first, when the Writer relates the General's attempt to fell a tree with a power saw, and, in the final scene, when the Writer confronts the General with the news of his fatal illness. Here, the scenes are not underscored by terminal silence, but by music. Music is a privileged art form throughout Bernhard's work. In his autobiographical volume *Der Atem* (*Breath*), he explains the important role music played in his battle against tuberculosis:

Ich dachte schon wieder an die Musik. Ich hörte schon wieder Musik in meinem Eckbett, Mozart, Schubert, Ich hatte schon wieder die Fähigkeit, aus mir heraus Musik zu hören, ganze Sätze. Ich konnte die in meinem Eckbett aus mir heraus gehörte Musik zu einem, wenn nicht zu *dem*	I thought again of music. I again heard music in my corner bed, Mozart, Schubert, I again had the ability, to hear music out of myself, entire compositions. I know that the music I heard out of myself was one of, if

wichtigsten Mittel meines Heilungsprozeßes machen. (1978; 46-47)	not *the* most important means of my recovery. process

In *The Ignoramus and the Madman*, *The Force of Habit*, *Minetti*, *The Lime Works*, and a number of other works, music possesses a miraculous perfection which is rationally inexplicable within their pessimistic presented worlds. The music is contrasted with the radical imperfection of all language, and shares the perfected formal completeness of silence. Given his belief in the failure of human activities, Bernhard does not even try to explain how Mozart was able to compose *The Magic Flute* (the key musical work in *The Ignoramus and the Madman*) or the "Haffner Symphony" (in *The Lime Works*), or how they can ever be successfully performed by mortals. Indeed, he differentiates between the beneficent effects of music on its audience, and the agony is causes its performers.

None of the characters in *The Hunting Party* perform the music themselves; they are too fragmented to do so, too limited, frustrated and obsessed. We hear the "Haffner Symphony" and Handel's "Suite No. 3 for Cembalo" played on the phonograph, ambassadors of beauty from another world. The pieces simultaneously represent a vision of harmonic completeness that contrasts with the cacophony of the stories being told, and represents a vision of universal form and coherence that can only be intuited when the characters face the entirety of their experience, which includes the knowledge of mortality. Unlike theatre, in which the referentiality of the work is always in question, music has no referent, and therefore exists as pure form. Bernhard repeatedly makes fun of the inevitable distortions of theatrical mimesis, as in the Christmas pageant the General praises because of its total verisimilitude; the Prince played a prince and the Princess played a princess, he tells us. The naïveté of the General's aesthetic is suddenly undercut when the General's wife recalls that her husband played God in that same pageant. Music, since it is not mimetic, is free of such distortions.

There is more than a little Schopenhauer haunting the pages of Bernhard, and the following lines of Schopenhauer's could easily be attributed to Bernhard:

> The unutterable depth of all music by virtue of which it
> floats through our consciousness as the vision of a paradise
> firmly believed in yet ever distant from us, and by which also
> it is so fully understood and yet so inexplicable, rests on the
> fact that it restores to us all the emotions of our inmost
> nature, but entirely without reality and far removed from
> their pain...How rich in content and full of significance the
> language of music is, we see from the repetitions as well as
> the *Da capo* the like of which would be unbearable in works
> composed in a language of words, but in music are very
> appropriate and beneficial, for, in order to comprehend it
> fully, we must hear it twice. (Schopenhauer 1891, I, 341-42)

Bernhard uses the frustration engendered by verbal repetition, in which every expression is a fiasco, and repetition merely the reiteration of compounded failures, with the beauty of Bach and Mozart, in which repetition is freed from frustration and becomes a source of beauty. He is saved from total, unrelenting pessimism by the mystery of music.

It is difficult to evaluate *The Hunting Party*. It eschews traditional dramatic structure, exhibits very little interaction between characters, either between speeches, or between the linguistic and the extralinguistic situations. By minimizing the potential manifestative and expressive qualities in the situation, the play tends toward stasis and opacity. According to the criteria I have established in the earlier chapters, it is not very dramatic. But it must be remembered that the term "dramatic" is descriptive rather than evaluative. An artist may choose to work within one artistic kind and yet mix it with qualities from other literary or theatrical kinds. The theatres of Kandinsky and Robert Wilson, for example, are closer to the visual arts than to dramatic literature. In *The Hunting Party*, and much of Bernhard's other dramatic work, it is only by minimizing conventional dramatic techniques that Bernhard's austere conflict between language and silence is able to emerge. The austerity and reiterative qualities of the text are essentially undramatic, but they are perhaps the most effective means for the expression of those qualities that stand at the center of Bernhard's artistic vision. *The Hunting Party* is static, closer to the lyric dramas of Yeats, Maeterlinck and Hofmannstahl, and the dramaticules of Beckett than to the more purely dramatic works of

Osborne and Bond. It stands eloquently in the undefined areas between theatre and closet drama, between music and silence.

FRAGMENTS OF THE INEXPRESSIBLE: "THE IRRATIONAL ARE DYING OUT"

Elam (1980, 114-117) has developed the very useful notion of *subworlds* in drama. This term refers to the states of affairs projected by various characters within a play, pertaining to their beliefs and hypotheses concerning the presented world. Some of these statements may be confirmed in the course of the play, others may be proven false, while still others may remain unconfirmed. A playwright can create tension through the establishment of conflicting subworlds. The murder mystery, for example, develops through a proliferation of subworlds, one of which is confirmed by the detective in the final scene, as the accurate description of the presented world. Subworlds can either directly conflict, as those of Mr. Combes and the peasants do in *Bingo*, or gradually be subsumed within a single, larger context, as in *The Hunting Party*. Individual subworlds can even contain their own conflicts and ambiguities, as we saw in *Véra Baxter*.

Peter Handke's *The Irrational Are Dying Out* (*Die Unvernünftigen sterben aus*) puts two distinct subworlds into conflict with each other; one of late capitalist economics and one of private memory and longing. They are brought together in the figure of Quitt, a magnate who also harbors within himself a perilous fascination with his own subjectivity. At length, he is defeated by his inability to live exclusively in either subworld.

Each subworld is defined by its own language. The first is that of the industrial magnates; the characters who control the presented world also control its language. Since all of the characters have access to that language, communication about financial matters is possible. It is the language of rationality, practicality, and materialism. It attempts to assimilate all reality into a method:

> Du weißt, was es bedeutet, wenn einer von uns menschlich wird oder gar vom Tod redet. Ein Gefühl wird bei uns nach dem ersten Schrecken zur Methode. (Handke 1973, 77)

> You know what it means when one of us becomes human or even speaks about death. An emotion, after the first moment of fright, becomes for us a method. (Handke 1976, 233)

The characters speak this language in complete sentences and in normal word order. The vocabulary is abstract, unemotional, and reveals few manifestative qualities. It aims to subsume all experience and order it productively. This is consistent with the actions of Quitt's fellow magnates, who come together in the first act to eliminate all competition, and work cooperatively. Each is to consult with the others on every business decision. Individualism, whether in business techniques or language, is seen as an impediment. It is the language of the conglomerate, the multinational corporation, and the cartel:

> Wir mußten investieren, die Steuer zwang uns dazu. Das brauche ich dir nicht zu erklären. Außerdem ist gerade eine Supermarkette der geeignete Umschlagsplatz. So haben wir unsere eigenen Verkaufsstellen und verlieren keine Rabatte an die Einzelhändler. (22)

> I had to invest, taxes forced us to. I don't have to explain that to you. And, besides, a big chain is just the right market for some of our products. That way we have our own outlets and don't need to discount to the retailers. (180)

Such disinterested conversation as this is, in itself, highly undramatic. It is rendered dramatic here only because it conflicts with the second language of *The Irrational Are Dying Out*, which is the highly personal language of subjective experience. This language is rich in manifestative qualities. It abounds in visual imagery, descriptions of emotions and physical sensations. It tends to be lyric and rhapsodic. Most importantly, however, it is characterized by disjunctiveness. When Quitt describes an event and his emotional reaction to it, both the event and the emotion are vividly expressed, unlike the language of business, which describes systems, rather than objects or emotions. In the language of business, objects only have value by virtue of their function within the whole; in the language of subjective experience, all perceptions have an innate value:

Und kürzlich sah ich einen Stummfilm. Man hatte keine Musik unterlegt, so war es meistens ganz still im Kino. Nur ab und zu, wenn es komisch wurde, lachten irgendwo ein paar Kinder und hörten gleich wieder auf. Auf einmal hatte ich ein Todesgefühl. Das Gefühl war so stark, daß ich die Beine weit auseianderstellte und die Finger spreizte. (44)	And recently I saw a silent film. No music had been dubbed in, so it was almost completely quiet in the theatre. Only now and then when something funny happened a few scattered children laughed and stopped again at once. Suddenly I had a sense of death. The feeling was so strong that I yanked my legs apart and spread my fingers. (201)

The language is highly concrete and specific, but the relationship between the elements is mysterious. Quitt's emotional experience does not proceed as the inevitable result of an external stimulus. One lacuna separates response (the feeling of death) from stimulus (the silent film), and another separates his emotion, from his physical manifestation of it. There is no explicit linguistic link between the film and the emotional experience: the phrase "auf einmal" [suddenly] only places the events in a temporal relationship, not a causal one. The emotional response gains vividness from its striking setting; the ominous mood is strengthened by the inexplicable gap between the setting and the emotion.

As a successful businessman in by day and a sentimental admirer of Adalbert Stifter by night, Quitt serves as the focus in this battle of opposed values and languages. He appears to be successful in both realms, and it is only when he allows his personal desires to disrupt the world of finance is he destroyed. Acting in accordance with his desire to assert himself as an irrational individual, he threatens the entire economic system. Driven to disrupt society by his asocial and individualistic impulses, he brings about a confrontation of the play's two linguistic systems. Without Quitt, there would be no conflict. He begins as an inhabitant of both realms, and ends as an isolated inhabitant in the world of subjective vision.

In this play, subjective experience exists autonomously of objectively existing reality. At the same time, subjective experience can have no effect on objective reality without translating itself into the objective and intersubjectively given sphere of language or action. Language is the primary mediator between the subjective and objective realms. It exists on the frontier between individual existence and society. Repeated verbal expressions of subjective experience are necessary, for without it there would be no way to make the spectator aware of a sphere of experience totally alien to the physical world of the setting. Since subjective experience cannot be founded in objectively presented events, it requires repeated verbal expression for its intersubjective foundation.

This quality of disjunction appears most obviously in the speech of Quitt's Wife that closes the first act. She has only spoken rarely up to this point, and very briefly. Since she has been wandering aimlessly across the stage throughout the act, the spectator expects that her speech may somehow clarify her behavior, which has not yet been accounted for. But her speech turns out to be only a series of fragments:

> Ich...wo das...weil nämlich...hm...*Sie räuspert sich*...und du...nicht wahr...*Sie lacht unschlüssig*...dies und das...und der Herbst...wie ein Stein...jenes Rauschen...die Ammoniten... und die Lehmklumpen an den Schuhsohlen. (56)
>
> I...where it...because ...hm...*(She clears her throat.)*...and you...isn't it...*(She laughs indecisively.)* ...this and that...and autumn... like a stone...that roaring...the Ammonites...and the mud on the soles of the shoes...(212)]

The speech communicates little more than her intense desire to say something, a desire that is blocked by the extreme disjuncture between the phrases. We are frustrated in our attempts to unite the fragments

The Irrational Are Dying out

into a coherent statement. The states of affairs are discontinuous. As with Quitt's experience in the movie house, his wife's statement manifests an emotion that cannot be analyzed, since it does not ground itself in external circumstances. Here, the language of subjective experience lacks any clear and unified set of referents.

This language of subjectivity is used by Handke for two different effects. The first, as seen above, is an indefinite juxtaposition of elements that can express an aura of dreamlike mystery, much like that found in surrealist art. The second is comic. Here, the disjunction between cause and effect can deflate the pretenses of the emotional expression:

Alles stand von mir abgewendet, in einer sanften Harmonie. Beim Scheißen hörte ich meine Geräusche dabei wie einem Unbekannten aus einer Nachbarkabine. (7)	Everything stood with its back to me, in gentle harmony with itself. While I was taking a shit I heard the sounds I was making as if they came from a stranger in the next cubicle. (166)

The use of the contrasting tones gives us two valuations of the world of subjective experience. The mysterious tone gives it a high valuation: we find such juxtapositions fascinating, in their suggestive elusiveness. The comic tone makes us laugh at the juxtaposition as a kind of affectation or silliness, in which the trivial is called upon to carry an disproportionately large weight of meaning. Handke introduces the world of subjective experience in the comic mode, only to modulate into the mysterious as the first act progresses. By maintaining both modes, Handke invites the spectator to entertain two possible valuations of this subworld.

Because the subjective world operates independently of the objective, it is possible to have discontinuous elements functioning simultaneously. For example, near the end of the play, Quitt strangles Kilb, but none of the speech during the murder refers to this action. Rather, Quitt recounts a memory of insomnia. Quitt's consciousness is split into two distinct and disconnected intentions. Different impulses do not war with each other; they simply co-exist. Both sequentially and simultaneously, the subworld of subjectivity moves toward the absolute sovereignty of each individual element.

It is for precisely this reason that the language of the magnates cannot subsume subjective experience. It serves no purpose, and cannot be articulated in relationship to anything else. It cannot be explained by the laws of economic determinism and causality. It is profoundly personal and asocial. When Quitt challenges Paula Tax to explain his experience in the movie house, she does not use a single word from his account in her response:

Ich kann es Ihnen mit keinen sozialen Bedingungen erklären. Es gehört bedingungslos Ihnen und ist nicht nachzuvollziehen. Als etwas Asoziales ist es der Rede nicht wert. Die Massen haben andre Sorgen. (44-45).	I can't explain it to you by social conditions. It is unconditionally yours and can't be emulated. As a social factor it's not worth mentioning. The masses have other worries. (200)

She disregards the experience because her language is inadequate to deal with it. It is, significantly, "nicht der Rede wert" [not worth mentioning]. Every language contains a potential range of world views, and events that defy that structure in any way, pose a threat to it. Handke has repeatedly dealt with the limitations a linguistic system forces on thought and perception, so much so that his plays have been treated as creative extensions of Wittgensteinian philosophy (Gilman 1974, 268-69). In *Kaspar*, Handke dramatized the process of language acquisition. As the title character learns to speak, he internalizes the platitudes and received wisdom of his society. By the end of the play, Kaspar has mastered the language, and become virtually indistinguishable from the other Kaspars who have come to populate the stage.

This is not to imply that Handke rejects all language as evil. Human beings require language for social intercourse, and to enable them to cope with the terrifying occurrences that surround them. Language provides a system that allows people to make sense of reality. The ultimate horror in Handke's dramatic universe is aphasia. Quitt's Wife buries her face in her hands after her unsuccessful attempt at communication with her husband. In *The Ride Across Lake Constance* [*Der Ritt über den Bodensee*], the characters, having undergone symbolic mutilation, are rendered totally aphasic. They cannot

The Irrational Are Dying out

communicate in any way; attempts at gestures are stillborn and attempts at speech terminate in inarticulate sounds. From *Kaspar* to his latest dramatic piece, *The Play of Questions* [*Das Spiel von Fragen*], characters try to orient themselves in a bewildering uniters through verbal acts. Speech is a means of reducing anxiety. As a result Handke's dramatic characters try to interpret every act verbally:

> KILB: Ich heiße Franz Kilb.
> HANS: *lacht*
> KILB: Gefällt Ihnen der Name nicht?
> HANS: Es ist etwas anderes. Ich habe nämlich gerade mit mir sel-ber gesprochen, fast fließend. Wir haben hier nichts gegen Namen. (11) .

> KILB: My name is Franz Kilb.
> (HANS *laughs*)
> Don't you likemy name?
> HANS: It's something else. I was talking to myself now--fluently almost. We don't have anything against names here. (169)

Kilb wants to know the meaning behind Hans's laugh, which is an ambiguous indication that Kilb interprets as the result of his introduction. He wants a less ambiguous verbal assertion to take its place. Hans, however, refuses the linguistic context Kilb has constructed for his laughter. He asserts that his act was autonomous; the sole audible fragment of an otherwise inaudible soliloquy. His internal world remains independent of Kilb's external stimulus. By defusing Kilb's highly personal affront with an absurdly bland generalization ("Wir haben hier nichts gegen Namen"), he reduces the challenge to his own autonomy to ridiculousness, and leaves Kilb still prey to his own sense of vulnerability.

The unverbalized is a threat. When language fails, panic ensues:

> KOERBER-KENT: Vielleicht können Sie ihn...*Er sucht das Wort*. Wie sagt man?
> QUITT: Beglückwünschen?
> KOERBER-KENT: Nein.
> QUITT: Beknien?

> KOERBER-KENT: Perhaps you could. . .him (*He tries to find the word*) What's the word?
> QUITT: Congratulate him?
> KOERBER-KENT: No.
> QUITT: Work on him?

KOERBER-KENT: So ähnlich...Nein.
QUITT: Zwischen die Knie nehmen?
KOERBER-KENT: *panisch* O Gott, was ist geschehen, ich finde das Wort nicht mehr, ich finde das Wort nichtmehr. Was hat man mit mir vor? Komm herab, Sonnenfinsternis! Schlag aus der Erde, Höllenfeuer! (85)

KOERBER-KENT: Something like that... no.
QUITT: Take him over your knees?
KOERBER-KENT: (*Panicstricken*) Oh, God, how did this happen? I can't find the right word any more. What are they doing to me? Come down, eclipse of the sun! Hellfire, burst forth from the earth! (241)

The effect is comic; a momentary lapse in articulateness becomes hyperbolically inflated into an apocalyptic occurrence. A failure of language elicits linguistic hysteria. The absence of a single word is enough to completely shatter Koerber-Kent's assured and practical stance.

The very ease with which the polite and official language of business negotiations can be blown sky-high for want of the proper word infuses the most impersonal expressions in *The Irrational Are Dying Out* with tension. The polite discourses of analysis and control are not the spontaneous expression of characters who feel nothing but rational impulses, but of irrational creatures who take great pains to combat the chaotic forces of anxiety within them, and to hide them from the outer world. The occasional expressions of intensely emotional and irrational impulses from these characters gradually establish an extralinguistic context of anxiety bordering on hysteria that comes to surround their most calm and measured pronouncements. The ferocity with which Von Wullnow reacts to Quitt's individualistic actions reveals both the abysses of passion within all of these characters and the deep threat posed to the magnates by Quitt's action. By violating their business agreement, Quitt has destroyed their expectations. If their expectations are false, anything can happen, and both rational analysis and comprehensible behavior become imperiled. Social and economic relationships, like language, are meant to insure stability and predictability. Quitt's action, therefore, disrupts their language, their social relationships, and their fundamental orientation to reality. Faced with a total threat, the magnates' usual calmness turns to panic and mindless vituperation:

> Ich verfluche dich! Wer deinen Namen vor mir ausspricht, dem greife ich un den Mund und reiße ihm die Zunge heraus, und zwar eigenhändig. Warte, ich trete dir jetzt auf den Fuß. *Er tut es, ohne daß Quitt reagiert. Er bläst die Wangen auf und schlägt sich selber darauf. Er beißt sich in den Handrücken. Er schlägt sich mit der Faust auf den Kopf--tupft sich plötzlich besorgt die Haare.* (75).
>
> I damn you! Whosoever utters your name before me, there shall I reach into his mouth and rip out his tongue, and with my very own hands, in fact. Wait, I'm going to step on your foot. (*He does so, not that* QUITT *reacts.* VON WULLNOW *blows up his cheeks and slaps them with his hands. He bites the back of his hand. He hits his head with his fist, quickly touches up his hair.*) (231)

Von Wullnow's anxiety leads to a rage that manifests itself through the complete deterioration of his rational discourse. His passion plunges him into a maelstrom of subjective indications. His extravagant description of what he will do to a person who mentions Quitt's name is not to be understood as a report of an actual event, but as a violent verbal image that express an extreme of violent rage. Each sentence in Von Wullnow's tirade (only a portion of which is quoted above) relates to his hatred of Quitt, and is thus unified on the extralinguistic level. Finally, words are no longer adequate to convey his passion, and he launches into a series of discrete gestures, all of which are unified only by the violence of their expression. He has temporarily lost his ability to form linguistic expressions, and can only indicate his psychic state. His hysterical rage takes him even to the point where his own intention breaks down, and the irrational intrudes into his own gestures as he touches up his hair, a visual *non sequitur* which bears no relationship to his anger. Quitt's act of betrayal momentarily shatters the linguistic world of Big Business, revealing the anxiety that lies beneath the veneer of its impersonal language.

The destructive potential of the language of irrationality however, is not to be underestimated, or merely seen as a threat to a particular ideological system. Language too is a system, that presupposes the existence of shared meaning. A system made up of absolutely unique phenomena is an impossibility. Therefore, the language challenges all the structures of culture. As *The Irrational Are Dying Out* reaches it conclusion, both the main text and the side text grow ever more fragmented. At the beginning of the second act, Quitt's hitherto realistic living room has unaccountably grown bizarre. A block of ice has replaced the sofa, a half-deflated hot-air balloon stands in place of the sandbag, and a large rock, a piano, children's drawings, and a glass trough filled with yeast complete the setting. None of the characters comment on this bizarre decor. There is no attempt to justify the set according to realistic expectations. Like the language of subjective experience, this set resists interpretation; it is an enigmatic configuration of disconnected objects. Through it, the presented world takes on qualities increasingly resistant to the viewer's rational interpretations. As the act proceeds, words and actions grow ever further apart from each other, until, at the end, we are left with the image of snakes writhing on the carpet. We have moved from the world of explanation to that of inexplicable phenomena. Blumer (1973, 127-33) has rightly drawn attention to Handke's affinity to the thought of Novalis in this play, which Blumer reads as a Romantic challenge to the "allzu vernünftige Wirklichkeit" [all too rational reality] of the modern world (Blumer 1973, 130). It must be added, however, that Handke's play offers no hope that a new intersubjectivity can be built on the foundation of this subjectivity. Its tendency is to grow ever more obscure and withdrawn. As Quitt delivers his final monologue he tries to stutter, an appropriate activity for someone who is moving away from the intersubjectivity of language.

All systems are threatened by the hermetic nature of subjectivity, and yet it cannot be totally effaced, even by its most ruthless opponents. Its anarchic presence, even in the most rational enterprises, makes itself felt in slips of the tongue, *non sequiturs*, synchronicity, jokes, dreams, and outbreaks of fantasy. The rational must always be on guard and anxious. This anxiety is shared by all the characters in the play, despite their other differences. The extralinguistic situation is charged with a shared quality of anxiousness that only occasionally expresses itself directly. In a performance of

The Irrational Are Dying Out, gestures, postures, and other physical indications of tension and anxiety will intensify this aspect of the presented world. The two opposed languages, of Quitt's Wife and the magnates, are ultimately grounded in a single extralinguistic context.

This play aptly illustrates Veltruský's observation (1976, 128-130) that linguistic links lead to clarification or explanation, while extralinguistic links lead to a chain of emotional reactions. The language of rationality in the play represents an attempt to order and explain events, and the language of subjective experience us an expression of emotional states. The opposing modes of discourse oppose the two basic modes of unifying the main text.

One specific verbal reaction to the anxiety experienced by all the characters is self-definition through language. The characters describe themselves, enumerate their qualities, relate their dreams, and tell anecdotes. Quitt, being the most reflective and melancholy character, talks about himself the most, but all of the characters participate in this activity somewhat. They share a need to verbalize their anxiety, not only because the verbalization reduces the anxiety, but because verbalization is the only way to make their personal experience accessible to others. These attempts at self-definition reveal the essential egocentricity of Handke's characters, one which far exceeds the egocentric tendencies of the characters in *Bingo* and *The Hunting Party*. In *Inadmissible Evidence*, there is a high degree of egocentric speech, but it is mostly spoken by the protagonist, rather than exhibited by all the characters. Handke is drawing on one of the most common attributes of human speech and drawing attention to its significance. Speech researches have found that 30 to 40 percent of all expressions uttered in adult conversation contain first person singular pronouns (Brown & Van Riper, 35). A similar study of a "typical American family" concluded that 81.3 percent of the expressions uttered contained references to the speakers (Brown and Van Riper, 35-36). The egocentric speeches of *The Irrational Are Dying Out* imply that speech is not only needed for us to understand events within our environment but are also needed for us to understand our own psychic states and acts, and to constitute our self-images:

> Every expression seeks to obtain the *recognition* of other people. I want to be known as I am, in my basic sincerity, to men and to God himself. I expect this recognition as a con-

firmation of my being and a contribution to my being. (Gusdorf 1965, 56)

The egocentric utterance both forms the speaker's identity and presents that identity to others for validation.

The desire for self-definition can be fulfilled through either of the two languages that we have observed at work in *The Irrational Are Dying Out*. Kilb describes himself according to his somewhat eccentric occupation, using the language of rationality. He accepts his position in capitalist society and describes himself in those terms. He acts in accordance with his social role, and does not exhibit any subtleties of characterization:

> Von jeder großen Aktiengesellschaft im Land besitze ich eine Aktie. Ich reise von Hauptversammlung zur andern und übernachte im Schlafsack. Ich fahre mit dem Rad, hier sehen Sie die Fahrradklammern, Ich bin ein Junggeselle in den besten Jahren, meine Reflexe funktionieren. (12) .

> I own one share of every major corporation in the country. I travel from one stockholders' meeting to the next and spend the nights in my sleeping bag. I go by bike--see, look at the trouser clips. I'm a bachelor in the prime of life, my reflexes function perfectly. (170)

Kilb's character is well-defined and static, staying within the boundaries of his own self-definition.

Quitt's character, on the other hand, allows himself to be amorphous. He does not present his social function through his speeches, but his subjective experiences, which are in continual flux and difficult to express. His vague terrors, longings, and melancholy moods resist cold, objective formulation. Even his address to his colleagues, broken down under six points, each enumerated in turn, progressively strays from rational statements into random observations. Like Quitt, his wife remains a figure who is characterized only by her lack of definition. The inner flow of experience cannot coalesce into a *Gestalt*. The language of rationality offers a relatively stable identity based on a social role. The language of the irrationality offers no identifiable core of social or psychological identity, only a flux of perceptions, dreams, and desires.

The reason the irrational are dying out is because the presented world contains no outlet for their subjectivity. Quitt asks his manservant to read him a passage from Adalbert Stifter's *The Old Bachelor* [*Das Hagestolz*]. The lengthy passage that Hans reads from that novella, filled with evocations of tender emotion, bring together the coherence and clarity of the rational language with the emotional depth and fullness of experience of the language of irrationality. Stifter's language allows subjective experience to become intersubjectively given. Stifter's expression of sentiments, Quitt believes, is an attenuated form of an earlier and more intense emotion, but it nevertheless remains evocative. Like the author-protagonist of Handke's novel, *Short Letter, Long Farewell* [*Der kurze Brief zum langen Abschied*], who travels across the United States with a copy of Gottfried Keller's *Green Heinrich* [*Der grüne Heinrich*] in his suitcase, Quitt is nostalgic for the vanished ability to communicate highly personal experience found in late nineteenth century fiction. Both Quitt and the narrator of *Short Letter, Long Farewell* find themselves in societies that are scarce on forms that embody such experiences. Both turn briefly to popular forms of expression; Quitt sings the blues and the narrator watches movies and visits John Ford. But these solutions are temporary and unsatisfactory; Quitt dies, and the novelist expresses his experiences in the first-person form of *Green Heinrich*. Neither is able to find a suitable contemporary form for their late Romantic self-absorption. Both of these characters concentrate on personal experience in an age that stresses collective experience. The America of *Short Letter* incarnates collective values that bewilder the narrator. In a collective society, the language changes in such a manner that the first-person narrative, so beloved of 19th century authors of *Bildungsromane* like Keller and Stifter, becomes an anachronism:

"Wir Amerikaner sagen 'wir', auch wenn wir von unseren Privatsachen reden," antwortete John Ford. "Das kommt villeicht daher, daß für uns alles, was wir tun, Teil einer gemeinsamen öffentlichen Aktion ist. Ich-

"We Americans says 'we,' even when we talk about private things," answered John Ford. "That probably comes from the fact that for us, everything we do, is part of a common public action. There are only I-stories,

> Geschichten gibt es nur dort, wo einer für alle anderen steht. Wir gehen mit unserem Ich nicht so feierlich um wie ihr." (Handke 1972, 188)
>
> where one stands for all the others. We don't go about so festively with our egos as you." [trans. RFG]

Ford, as artist and American, is able to reconcile artistic vision and contemporary values. Handke's protagonists are too thoroughly creatures of the Old World to share Ford's successful synthesis, and their discontent with the modern world often takes the form of nostalgia.

Quitt, knowing no other outlet, unleashes his Romantic egoism in the modern realm of corporate finance. Paula diagnoses what she believes to be the limitations of Quitt's personal vision:

> Sie sprechen nämlich von sich wie der Stellvertreter des Allgemeinen. Was sie persönlich erleben, wollen Sie für uns alle erleben. Ihr privat geschwitzes Blut bringen Sie uns Verstockten zum Opfer. Ihr Ich will mehr als es selbst sein [...](37-38)
>
> Because you're talking about yourself like the deputy of universal truth. What you experience personally you want to experience for all of us. The blood you swear in private you bring as a sacrifice to us, the impenitent ones. Your ego wants to be more than itself [...] (195)

Quitt values his uniqueness too highly, Paula argues. In Riesman's (1950) terms, he is an "inner-directed" character in an "other-directed" age. Quitt, in rebellion against the agreement he has made with his peers to terminate competition in favor of cooperation, rebels against the idea of "fair trade" in an age of conglomerates and multinational corporations. Fair trade is an other-directed value, since it exalts favorable peer relationships over personal achievement:

> The word *fair* in part reflects a carry-over of peer-group values into business life. The peer-grouper is imbued with the idea of fair play; the businessman, of fair trade. Often this means that he must be willing to negotiate matters on which he might stand on his rights. (Riesman 1950, 160)

As a figure of ruthless individualism in commerce, Quitt harks back to the robber barons of the late nineteenth and early twentieth centuries, the inner-directed tycoons who believed in free trade and sought neither peer approval or cooperation--Vanderbilt, Carnegie, Morgan, and the fictional tycoons of Dreiser and Sternheim. Quitt is as much an anachronism in his financial affairs as he is in his literary preferences.

But Quitt's dilemma is not only a problem of a Romantic anachronism in the contemporary world. Hans-George Gadamer has neatly summarized the larger dilemma:

> One will find a conflict between the continuing tendency toward individualization in language and that tendency which is just as essential to language, namely, to establish meanings by convention. For to be sure, the fact that one can never depart too far from linguistic conventions is clearly basic to the life of language. But on the other hand, he who only speaks a language in which conventionality has become total in the choice of words, in syntax, and in style forfeits the power of address and evocation that comes solely with the individualization of a language's vocabulary and of its means of communication. (Gadamer 1976, 86-87)

One extreme of individualization is represented by Quitt's Wife, whose fragmented statements and aimless wanderings indicate a desire to communicate an inner experience that remains opaque to the spectator. At the other extreme stands the manservant, Hans, who admits, at the beginning of the play, that he has nothing to say about himself and does not dream. His language is a medium of social exchange, lacking individualized expression. As such, he is as complete an example of the rational as the magnates are. Rationality and irrationality cut across class boundaries.

Quitt's linguistic dilemma can be understood more fully if we return briefly to the phenomenology of expressions which has been presented in the first chapter of this study. Personal, subjective experience is prelinguistic and founds our linguistic acts. Since language is a shared system of generalized meanings, however, it can never totally fulfill the uniqueness of any prelinguistic state or action. There is always a discrepancy between the unique experience and the verbal expression of it. As a result, none of Quitt's experiences become fully exhibited to us. Handke stresses the discrepancy between experience and expression by having Quitt express his sense of self in vague, generalized, and often clichèd statements. His very first expression, "Ich bin heute traurig (2)" [I feel sad today (165)] sounds superficial and banal; it is unable to manifest the state it describes in its full complexity. The psychic state of the character, lacking both outward verification in external circumstances and complete communication in verbal expression, remains isolated within the character. Instead of being able to intuit Quitt's experiences in their full complexity, the spectator is led to examine Quitt's inevitably incomplete attempts at personal expression, and perceive the anxiety and melancholy that underlie those attempts.

Unable to verbally communicate his inner experiences Quitt takes action. His rebellion against the contemporary world attempts to mediate between the subjective and objective realms: "Es wird blitzen, und die Vorstellung wird Wirklichkeit sein" (55) [There will be lightning and thunder, and the idea will become flesh (211)]. Quitt wishes to become the *logos*, the omnipotent mediator between idea and reality. But his action is no more successful than his attempts at speech. It is only perceived as a treacherous and economically irresponsible action by his colleagues. The system of economic exchange is a far less successful medium for personal expression than the linguistic system is. It is a conventionalized system without the potential for individualization.

Quitt's failures drive him into the isolated space of his apartment. Like the law office of *Inadmissible Evidence* and the bedroom of *Bingo*, the stage set of *The Irrational Are Dying Out* finally becomes a space of the protagonist's isolation and self-absorption. In this play, however, the transformation of the physical setting mirrors the gradual domination of the protagonist's consciousness over the presented world, as described in the side text. Even though the characters in the presented world do not seem to perceive this transformation, we do, and the odd disjunctions between realistic setting and surrealist objects, as well as between setting and plot incident, take us further into the world of the irrational. We are made increasingly aware of the strangeness of Quitt as his vision progressively dominates the presented world. In other words, the side text gradually narrows the gap between the objectively existing set, composed of real objects, and the intangible world of the protagonist's emotions. Quitt's vision is vindicated, despite his death, insofar as the stage setting comes to conform to his vision rather than Von Wullnow's. Although the setting never succeeds in rendering Quitt's vision accessible to the spectator's rational tendencies to interpretation and analysis, it satisfies the desire for the oneiric and mysterious. It is certainly a great advance over Quitt's "Ich bin heute traurig (7)" [I feel sad today (165)].

he action of *The Irrational Are Dying Out*, like that of *Inadmissible Evidence*, is a gradual elaboration of the first utterances of the protagonist. The general development, however, is reversed in the two plays. In *Inadmissible Evidence*, the text moves from the highly emotional and disjunctive speeches of Maitland to a gradual clarification of the situation, which is expressed in more linguistically unified speeches. In *The Irrational Are Dying Out*, the banalities of the opening slowly give way to greater intensity and greater linguistic disjunction. The play leads to ever more complex expressions of insatiable yearning.

The ending of the play reveals an unresolved tension between Quitt's death and his deepening vision. He is vindicated as the world comes to mirror his vision of it, even though he dies. On the rational level, Quitt's demise is due to the fact that he is an anachronism in the social and economic world of the play. On the irrational level, on which there are no relationships between phenomena, his death is experienced but incomprehensible.

The fact that irrationality need not be fatal is seen in the character of Hans, Quitt's manservant, who is strengthened by his master's foray into the irrational. At first, he is unable to remember anything personal about himself. After his employer's treachery, however, he is able to dream and remember personal details, and even fantasize about changing the world. Schlueter (1981, 344) is right to see him as Quitt's more hopeful alter ego, though it is important to note that it is Quitt's demise, not Hans' triumph, that dominates the close of the play, and that Hans' fantasies do not result in action. There is an unresolved tension in Hans' final soliloquy, as he both asserts that his world is changing, and his desire to do nothing but dream. His rhymed couplets point toward a closed poetic form, but the last line remains unrhymed and, therefore, unresolved. Handke is working his way toward a union of the rational and irrational, but the way is groping, tentative, and far from complete. Hans leaves the stage, and the spectacle of further fragmentation continues. Handke's sympathies lie on the side of subjective experience which underlies the actions of even the most rational and pragmatic characters and is occasionally expressed in their speeches. Existential anxiety here is fundamental and persists despite historical change. The thematic center of *The Irrational Are Dying Out* can be found in the following exchange between Paula and Quitt, as she dismisses his anxieties as trivial:

> PAULA: [...] Die Massen haben andre Sorgen.
> QUITT: Die aber vorübergehen werden?
> PAULA: Ja, weil auch die Bedingungen vorübergehen werden.
> QUITT: Und dann werden die Massen vielleicht meine Sorgen haben, die nicht vorübergehen. (44-45)

> PAULA: [...] The masses have other worries.
> QUITT: But which will pass.
> PAULA: Yes, because the conditions will pass too.
> QUITT: And then perhaps the masses will have my worries, which do not pass. (201)

Paula does not respond to Quitt's observation, to the possibility that existential problems are more enduring than social ones.

Handke's distrust of social analysis and rational models of human existence appears in his critical statements as well as his plays and fiction. When asked by *Theatre Heute* to evaluate the writings of Bertolt Brecht, Handke argued that they were far inferior to the writings of Shakespeare, Chekhov, Faulkner, Beckett, or Ödön von Horváth (1968, 28). Brecht, he contends, schematizes reality to the point where it ceases to be a valid model of experience; we all know that our experiences are far richer and more contradictory than Brecht presents them. Von Horváth, on the other hand, creates speeches that seem to spring from the inner complexities of the psyche itself and defy resolution. Handke's Brecht, is like Paula Tax, who rejects Quitt's experiences because they do not conform to her analytical model.

Indeed, it is possible to view *The Irrational Are Dying Out* as a refutation of the Brechtian theory of drama. Rainer Nägele and Renate Voris (1978, 92-96) are correct in observing that Quitt bears more than a passing resemblance to Brecht's ruthless and sentimental capitalist in *Saint Joan of the Stockyards*, but they try to interpret Quitt as merely a less sharply focused version of Mauler, and wrongly conclude that Handke's portrait is simply less effective than Brecht's. But Quitt's experiences cannot be dismissed as mere capitalist aberrations, whereas Mauler's sentimentality is presented clearly as a function of his bourgeois mentality and is, therefore, rooted in the economic realities of Brecht's presented world in that play. There, all character traits are founded in an analyzable socio-economic context. Handke is arguing from just the opposite position; the most central impulses of human nature cannot be reduced to a method of economic analysis. Nägele and Voris interpret the play through Paula's subworld of rational, social analysis, and are unable to come to terms with the triumph of the irrational in the side text. Schlueter (1981, 339-340) more accurately sees the play as the continuation of Handke's aesthetic concerns (though to link it to the work of Georg Lukács may still be overly "rational").

The Irrational Are Dying Out gradually replaces the objective world with subjective vision; the presented space becomes one that rejects the outside world. Even the belching of the new monster outside the apartment is founded in Quitt's imagination; it is the aural presentation of an image in one of Quitt's earlier speeches (101-103). The stage space becomes increasingly self-referential. Handke is interested in the erection of self-referential construct, not the explanation of a socio-economic processes. The construct intimates the presence of the psychic state, without ever analyzing it, or even overtly describing it. Handke is not interested in how Quitt wins control of the market, as Brecht would be. He is developing an aesthetic whose presuppositions are directly opposed to the materialism of Brecht and his epigones.

The Irrational Are Dying Out reveals the contest between modes of discourse, two visions of humanity, two kinds of drama. Handke slowly reveals the superiority of one mode of discourse, a discourse which attracts the theatrical spectator because it is potentially richer in manifestative qualities. The action of the play and the developing *mise en scène* further strengthen the claims of subjective experience over those of the contemporary world. Quitt's desire for self-expression is strong enough to enlist the our empathy, and lead us to share in his dilemma and see it, to a degree, as our own. *The Irrational Are Dying Out* investigates the gap between the pre-linguistic state and language, finally asserting the primacy and unintelligibility of the former. In favoring such radical subjectivity, however, Handke finds himself at an impasse by the end of the play, where there is no longer any conflict, any main text, or any intersubjectively given system of meaning. We are left with snakes writhing on the carpet, and the feeling that perhaps drama, along with the irrational, has died out. Perhaps Handke felt the same way: after finishing this play, nine years elapsed before another play of his appeared.

VAMPING WITH DAD:
"A PRELUDE TO DEATH IN VENICE"

No playwright in this volume has challenged the traditional format of the dramatic text more than playwright-director Lee Breuer. In his work with Mabou Mines, he has developed a style of playmaking that has been labeled one of the key examples of the "Theatre of Images" (Marranca 1977). Eschewing the traditional privilege of the main text over the side text, Breuer published his *Red Horse Animation* in 32 color plates, highly reminiscent of a comic book. The main text exists within a figurative composition, rather than against the whiteness of the printed page, and words and visual images augment each other. The method of presentation shows the importance of the visual aspects of Breuer's work, in which the words of the main text are not always the dominant element of the script.

Even in his works that find a more traditional form of presentation on the page, such as *A Prelude to Death in Venice*, Breuer puts great emphasis on the visual aspects of the production, prefacing the main text with 3 1/2 pages of side text, entitled "Playwright's Note," which covers aspects of sound, acting, set, lighting, and effects. The status of this preface, is, however, ambiguous. It stands in the printed text before the title of the play, which seems to give it some priority, as a staging that must be kept in mind while reading the play. Yet the side text of the play informs us that the Note "is not meant to encroach upon the director's province. It documents one set of solutions to the problems of staging posed by the text" (Breuer 1982, 11). Here Breuer makes a distinction between his roles as playwright and director, asserting his control in the printed text over the former, while limiting himself to making tactful, albeit copious, suggestions about the latter. Although the Theatre of Images tends to blur the distinction between director and playwright in its working methods, Breuer makes a gesture of dividing them along traditional lines in this text.

The main text is divided between two performers, referred to in the side text as "Actor" and "Voice." Each of these performers in turn plays multiple roles. The Actor plays himself (Bill) and an agent (Bill Morris), as well as operates a puppet (John Greed). The Voice plays all of the various voices we hear over the phone, as well as a member of the New York Police Department. By having each performer play several roles, Breuer not only foregrounds the theatricality with which the world of *Prelude* is being presented, but also suggests a multiplicity of identities within a single performer. Whereas the other playwrights in this study have all assigned only one role to each actor, assuming a fundamental unity underlying all the actions of a character, even when that character was enigmatic (Véra Baxter) or conflicted (William Shakespeare), Breuer begins with the assumption of a multiplicity of discrete psychic entities within each person:

> I believe firmly in the archetypal imagery, in the idea of control by the ancestors, in the idea that you are given a voice, that a character is simply an aspect of the *persona* of yourself, that you are never one thing, that you are constantly giving off energy the way an atom would radiate. (1982, 28)

The protean nature of the performer becomes an image, not of a specialized set of skills, but of our own multiple nature.

The most important division of roles is that of the Actor, who plays himself and operates John. The introduction of a puppet as a major character heightens our awareness of pairing. Since the puppet speaks, and endows phonic material with meaning, we tend to identify it as a human being like us. This tendency is furthered by its human form. But at the same time, we are aware that it is an inanimate object, and that our impulse to pair is incorrect. Both the comic and sinister aspects of the puppet come from our simultaneous perception of it as both human and inanimate. In *Prelude*, the resultant sense of uncanniness is heightened by the fact that we see Bill operating John, which is a constant reminder that John's autonomy is an illusion derived from the actions of Bill. Although both Bill and John are characters within the presented text, their ontological status in performance are not equal; Bill's actions give the illusion of autonomy and independence, while John's actions seem heteronomous and derived. The play moves from John's dominance to Bill's.

For the first four pages of the printed text, all of the main text is given to John and the words of the Voice over the two pay telephones. Bill appears as the silent puppeteer, only addressed by John when he needs more change for the phones. John's verbal energy is high; his expressions are short, often sentence fragments, and his language is colloquial, even slangy. At first, we can't hear the other end of the conversations, and have to construct the entire context on the basis of John's words alone. This task is made more difficult because John divided in his focus; he operates both phones at once, trying to keep two conversations going at a time. One is with an organization called "Johns Anonymous," which has given John its manual to read, and which John refuses to "do" something with. The other is with some acquaintance that John was going to drop in on, until he learns that the other person has gotten kittens without telling him. Both conversations are cryptic, and are made even more difficult to understand by the fact that they keep interrupting each other. They combine, however, to give us a sense of high comic energy and verbal aggressiveness:

> Hi. Sorry. I can't do it. I read that book. Right...the J.A. manual. That's a lucid book. You know what I'm saying? That's a work book. Right. It's about work--you know what I'm saying, "No!" Right. I'm saying, "No!" You know what I'm saying? My thing is not about work, my thing is about a vacation. In my life, at a critical juncture, I vowed not to work another day in my life. No. That's not the point. The point is, "I can work, but, I can only work when it's a vacation from a vacation." You know what I'm saying, "I can't do it!" It just ain't tourism (12).

The first "it" has no antecedent, but, unlike the antecedentless pronouns of *Véra Baxter*, it is neither reiterated nor set off with pauses. Any question about what "it" refers to is quickly swept away in the rapid-fire speech that follows, which is made up of short, simple, often repeated elements. The repetition of "You know what I'm saying" gives the character a certain aggressiveness, especially since his message is simple--"No." Breuer establishes a comic tone through the discrepancy between the simplicity of the message and the verbosity through which it is communicated. The comedy is strengthened by a metalinguistic joke, as the statement "You know what I'm saying, 'No!'" seems to be taken literally as a question by the interlocutor, and is answered, leading John to repeat the statement again "Right. I'm saying 'No.'" The language is quickly moving toward nonsense, as John first sets up an opposition between two elements, "vacation" and "work," only to collapse the opposition when he explains that he *can* work if "it's a vacation from a vacation." The speech ends with a final comic spin given to the notion of "vacation," as John identifies having a vacation with the business that derives from people's vacations, "It just isn't tourism." This is another conflation of the notions of work and vacation, and once again subsumes recreation under the category of work.

The quickness of the word play here leads to a constantly shifting of the states of affairs; oppositions are projected only to be turned on their heads or canceled out. Sentences are also rendered comic because they simultaneously refer to two very different states of affairs simultaneously. The conversation about the cats, for example, becomes comic because John says "When did you have kittens?" and "You had kittens" (12). There are two states of affairs here: one, projecting possession of cats; another, drawing on a slang expression, indicating that the person was very upset. Neither of these states of affairs proves to be important for the understanding of later action in *Prelude*. What is important is the comic tone conveyed by the double meaning, and the introduction of linguistic playfulness as an end in itself.

For *A Prelude to Death in Venice* abounds in verbal play, which foregrounds the very properties of the language, rather than simply using it as a transparent means to convey information or manifest psychic states. The most obvious is the double identification of "Venice," as both a city in Italy and a city in California. The verb "shoot" is used as both as an action performed with a gun and a camera, as well as a slang term for talking ("O.K. Shoot!" "Shooting the shit"). "John" functions as a proper name, a male in a casual sexual encounter, and a toilet. Some of these puns prove to be central to the structure of the work, as we shall see. Others are ornamental, like the reference to "having kittens." Just as Breuer foregrounds the theatricality of his play by using puppets and doubling, so too, he foregrounds the linguistic material of the main text by punning. Both techniques help to establish the presented world as one that does not effortlessly refer to states of affairs outside the play, but to an increasingly private and self-referential world.

Outside of the speaker at "Johns Anonymous," John's interlocutors at first are anonymous, and his relationship to them is vague. The states of affairs are vague, and our focus is more on John's rapid manipulation of two phones and sets of conversations. His use of the phones is compulsive; no sooner has one conversation ended then he is dialing another call, while still holding someone else on the other line. Ironically, we do not hear his live interlocutors, only the recorded messages on answering machines, rendering the mechanical voices more present than the living ones. This is an appropriate strategy for this part of the play, in which the inanimate character, the puppet, does all the speaking, and his human operator is silent. The main text of *Prelude* begins with voices that are cut off from their origins, projected through mechanical intermediaries, and the language is manic and confused.

The first of John's interlocutors to be clearly defined is his mother. His language suddenly becomes more sexual, introducing an Oedipal situation that will structure the remainder of the piece. Marranca (1979, 86) has observed that Breuer's *Animations* invite two distinct critical approaches to be brought into play, the psychoanalytic and the mythic. Here, the two approaches are brought together, as Breuer utilizes the central myth of psychoanalytic literature, that of Oedipus.

John insists that he loves his mother, despite the fact that he's getting ready to leave on vacation. These protestations of affection, however, are studded with obscenity. He insists he does "have a heart on"(15)--an odd expression, which punningly alludes to the more common vulgarism, "have a hard on." He tells his mother not to come and see him because "I've been a closet mother fucker for years and I'm not about to come out now" (15). Affection quickly becomes redefined as the most brutal expression of incest, and his rejection of his mother speaks far more loudly than any loving reassurances. The intertwining of two conversations, one in which he rejects his mother in sexual terms; the other, in which he looks forward to a vacation, lead us to infer that the vacation is a flight from incest with the mother, the very fear that led Oedipus to flee from Thebes.

This Oedipal configuration is further elaborated with the next caller, John's answering service, with a message from John's father. With this call, John is immediately threatened and Bill begins to grow in power. Even before the service announces that the message is from John's father, John hesitates to answer it, and Bill, with his first line, urges John to take it. The shift in power suddenly grows much more extreme as John asks for the message:

> JOHN: O.K. Shoot!
> (PHONE II *receiver shoots* JOHN *in the head.*)
> BILL: (*To "dead"* JOHN) Alas, poor john...(*To audience*) Hang on a sec...*
> BILL: (*On* PHONE II) Pop, don't shoot the talent. It's very expensive to repair. I'm speaking frankly; you do--and we sue.
> BILL: (*To audience*) Sorry. Hang on a sec...
> (BILL *brings* JOHN *back to life* [...] (16)

Thematically, the scene depicts an Oedipal catastrophe; the son, fleeing from the mother, nonetheless incurs the deadly wrath of the father. Stylistically, though, Breuer mitigates the horror by playing the passage as the broadest farce. It begins with a pun, as an invitation to speak ("Shoot") is mistaken as a command to fire a gun. The gun, in a second comic misplacement, is replaced by a telephone receiver, and shoots a puppet, who is mourned in Shakespearian parody. The puppeteer suddenly takes over the scene with the "death" of the puppet, directly addressing the audience for the first time in the play, and using the refrain that has become comic as John used it again and again in his multiple phone conversations ("Hang on a sec.") The threatening father is quickly put in his place verbally ("Pop"), and commanded to leave his son alone. Breuer minimizes any worry about John's life, by having Bill project a state of affairs in which John is not a character, but an object to be repaired. Bill "brings John back to life," and the play continues, as if nothing had happened.

Although this incident has not altered the causal sequence of events in the least, it has set up the presented world as one in which

Oedipal myth operates with lethal consequences. It provides the beginning of a gradual transition from a comic world to a somber world, permeated with death.

This lethal confrontation with the father makes John's next conversation with his mother very different than the earlier one. Gone is the sexual abusiveness and distance. He refers to her twice with the childish term "Mummy" (16). The father's violence toward the son is situated against an increasingly mythic horizon as John explains that the father wants to "shoot in Greece" (16). The myth is skewed, however, in John's account of it, "I'm supposed to kill my mother and marry my father" (16). The inversion is comic in its expression, but serious and central to the action of the play, since the play constructs a Freudian revision, in which it is the mother who is shunned and the father who is pursued. This mythic inversion continues the strategies that Marranca noted in the *Animations*, which "work to demystify stereotypical attitudes about malehood" (1979, 85).

So far, *A Prelude to Death in Venice* has exhibited no clear linguistic links to Thomas Mann's text, as the title of the play has led us to expect. The setting has been New York City, not Munich or Venice; John Greed is a far cry from Mann's dignified bourgeois artist, Gustav von Aschenbach; the broad, energetic, comic style contains no echoes of the "deliberate classicism" (Reed 1974, 174) that characterize Mann's novella. Breuer's allusions thus far have been to Sophoclean material, as transmitted to modern culture through Freud. But *Death in Venice* suddenly erupts into Breuer's text, with a message from the novelist himself.

No sooner does John make the first clear reference to Mann's work, explaining that he does not want to "shoot in Greece," as his father wishes, but "shoot in Venice," his answering service announces that "Tom" called. The identity of this caller is not clear until the service gives his number as "Eighteen seventy-five to nineteen fifty-five" (17). Breuer is assuming that his audience knows that these are the life dates for Thomas Mann, and that he is the author of *Death in Venice*. He further assumes that the audience is acquainted with at least the novella's plot.

Mann is identified with the father from the first. Both messages are announced by Mercury Message, Mercury being not only the messenger of the Olympians, but, in his role as Hermes Psychopompus, the conductor of souls into the Underworld, a figure of some importance in the iconography of *Death in Venice* (Reed 1962, 173). The build up to Mann's message is the same as to the father's; John asks for a pencil, then says "O.K. Shoot" (16, 17), but this time, as if to comically underscore the danger, John aims the receiver at the audience.

But the receiver doesn't go off. Instead, we hear the answering service, imitating Thomas Mann reading an abridged version of part of his novella. The long, virtually uninterrupted reading, with its long, elegant periods, contrasts with Greed's short, frantic bursts of speech. Greed is silent, no longer trying to carry on dual conversations. The introduction of Thomas Mann's voice is a radical departure from the main text up to this point, and its significance, so far only justified by the title, is not yet clear. A narrative projection of an unfolding set of states of affairs, seemingly independent of the previous main text, are projected.

Breuer does not select one of the famous passages describing Aschenbach in Venice, in the presence of Tadzio, but from the opening section, which describes the event that motivates Aschenbach's journey to Venice. It is a 'prelude,'or as Heller has so elegantly described it, "An overture which contains *in nuce* the whole drama and yet is the beginning of the story proper"(1961, 101). In it, we are told how Aschenbach, the renowned and highly disciplined author, goes for a walk because he is unable to relax after a morning of writing. Mann immediately presents us with a strange state of affairs. His writer does not have to discipline himself in order to write; rather, he is unable to check "the onward sweep of the productive mechanism within him" (17) [dem Fortschwingen des produzierenden Triebwerks in seinem Innern (Mann 1966, 444)]. This productive movement, "in which according to Cicero, eloquence resides" (17) [worin nach Cicero das Wesen der Beredsamkeit besteht (444)], is translated into physical movement. At length he finds himself before a mortuary chapel, on whose steps suddenly appears a young man. The contemplation of this figure releases in Aschenbach the image of a lush, primeval swamp, and a desire to travel, that leads him to Venice, Tadzio, and death

Although Breuer condenses the passage somewhat throughout, only one condensation is important enough to merit discussion here. He deletes Mann's lengthy description of the man on the chapel steps, and substitutes the appearance of the mute figure of Tadzio. This is not only a condensation, but a re-writing of Mann's narrative. The snub-nosed traveler, whether identified with Hermes (Reed 1974, 1973), "a Dürer image of Death" (Heller, 103), or a satyr-figure (Hayes & Quinby, 167), is identified with the gondolier and other sinister characters who later appear in Venice, not with the classically beautiful Tadzio. Breuer situates Tadzio's first appearance at the beginning of the novella, bringing out from the first the homosexual theme that only gradually unfolds in Mann's novella.

The side text tells us that the appearance of Tadzio, along with music by Bach and lighting effects "conspire to seduce JOHN" (18). There is a triple seductiveness here; of death (as articulated in Mann's passage), of male beauty (in the figure of Tadzio), and of high art (Mann and Bach). John, up to this point so unlike Aschenbach, becomes linked to him as a common victim of seduction by these forces, though he struggles against the fate scripted for him by Mann. He hangs up the phone, cutting short Mann's message, and returns to the first lines of the main text, as he calls "Johns Anonymous." This time, however, he's unable to get the number, and is only able to talk to "Johns" because they call him. The reason for his call is unclear, but the call itself, a rambling comic monologue, is the history of an addiction to film, a parody of the confessions made at an Alcoholics Anonymous meeting.

John confesses to being defined by pre-existing narratives; "I don't write my scripts," he explains (19). He is, rather, "a reactive system," constituted by other tellers. A dog projected Cocteau's *Beauty and the Beast* on him, leading him to conclude "I was not some 'Tom' 'Dick' or 'Harry.' No, I was a 'Jean'" (19). We are back to John's restless, energetic language, which now calls to mind the restlessness that led Aschenbach to take his walk. It also elaborates, through allusions, a homosexual matrix for John, rather than the earlier, incestuous and heterosexual one. The film projected on him was directed by Jean Cocteau, and the star in the film was Cocteau's lover, Jean Marais. This projection (and the word registers both as a cinematic and psychoanalytic term) leads John to perceive he is a "Jean." The joke works because "Jean" is nothing more then the French version of his name, but the resonance of a film that testifies to a famous gay relationship and leads its viewer to recognize himself in it (whether as the director or actor), restates the earlier seduction of John in a comic mode.

The confession mixes inside with outside, as John is both projected on and projecting. Everything becomes a potential screen and a potential projector. John becomes indistinguishable from a movie camera, as he refers to "my aperture," "my lens," "my sprocket holes" (19). Aschenbach's "productive movement" is conveyed through mechanical imagery, as Aschenbach's writing is transformed into filming.

John's addiction finds a response in "Johns Anonymous," who tells a story of another productive mechanism gone berserk, this time a sexual one. It is again a parody, but the tone is quiet and controlled now, rather than manic. The sentences are complete and well-formed, and the narrative is in the past tense. Only the frequent reiteration of a single obscene word ruptures the decorum of the speech. The comedy comes from using the formulae of alcohol and drug addiction to discuss sex:

> I made promises to myself, my family, my friends...and broke them. Short dry spells ended in heavy fucking. I tried to hide my fucking by going places where I was unlikely to see anyone I knew. Remorse was always with me. The next steps were closet fucking and excuses for trips to fuck without restraint--what it does to a person is apparent to everyone but the person involved. (21)

The monologue builds in moralizing extravagance. "Fucking," like filming in John's monologue, becomes an intransitive activity. There is no indication whether John's sexual partners were male, female, bestial--if indeed there were any partners at all. The hidden, unconsummated sexual longing of *Death in Venice* is inverted into lust erupting without object.

John Greed pays no attention to this testimonial. He is already on the other phone, trying to place a call to a friend in Luxembourg, who he thinks can help him with his vacation--Lieba Stoed. Here, Greed's projected vacation begins to take on the same goal as Aschenbach's, a union of Eros and Thanatos. His quest is interrupted by the police, who ask if Bill's seen a puppet who just charged a call to Luxembourg to the Fourth Precinct. The idea is outrageous enough to be amusing, but John reacts to it with the same anxious reaction that his father's message evoked; he calls his mother, and is so eager to speak to her that he starts speaking to her even before she answers the phone. The police's voice is, of course, spoken by the same performer as played the Mercury Messenger Service, who brought both the messages from the father and Thomas Mann. They are linked as figures of law and order, from which John seeks protection from the mother.

To approach the mother, however, is to run the threat of incest, and she begins to make sexual advances. His language grows in anxiety, "Don't Mummy...Please! No, not again. Don't do it..."(23). The assured, aggressive language of the beginning have disappeared completely, and we hear a pleading, terrified child.

As before, a conversation with the mother is followed by a call from the father. This time, an important addition is made to his condition; he is dead, and calling from the cemetery. The connection is made with Aschenbach's experience at the cemetery, since the father's extension at Forest Lawn is 666, the number of the Beast of *Revelation*, which John recognizes. He is identified, therefore, with the "two apocalyptic beasts" (18) [beiden apokalyptischen Tiere (445)] in front of the chapel. Breuer revises the chapel scene again; now it is not a middle-aged man seeing a youth who sets him on a journey of love and death, but a son who sees his father. The Oedipal scenario is beginning to be re-read through *Death in Venice*. Hayes and Quinby (1989, 163-64) have drawn attention to the trace of a father-son identification in the Aschenbach/Tadzio relationship, with Aschenbach described as the father who has no son, and Tadzio as the son who travels without a father, but what was at most subliminal in Mann becomes overt and central for Breuer.

The father's call disconcerts John, who, for the first time, has Bill answer the phone for him, as "Bill Morris," his agent. Bill takes over the role of the producer, talking in a parody of a hard-driving and successful member of the entertainment industry. He then talks to the mother, not whining as John did, but boasting that he can work miracles: "I can 'produce' reality" (25).

Once John relinquishes the phone to Bill, he goes mute. Bill, the silent puppeteer of the beginning, has a new, confident persona, that of Bill Morris. In time, he drops that, and speaks to the mother in his own voice. It is clear that we are to see Bill and John as aspects of a single character, not only by the way they have been staged, but by the fact that Bill continues to speak to the living mother and dead father as his parents. He also ties himself into the theme of relentless productivity, as he tells his mother, quoting Mann, "We don't want the 'rest' of history. We want 'that motus animi continuus in which, according to Cicero, eloquence resides'"(26).

As Bill comes into his own voice, John is no longer needed. Bill separates himself from the puppet with his teeth, rendering him an object without the semblance of life, dances with him, bites his neck like a vampire, and lays him down on the curb. With this, *Prelude* brings a third literary figure into play; after Oedipus and Aschenbach, Dracula. Where the image of Tadzio had once appeared, we see the figure of Dracula, whom Bill addresses as "Pop" (26). As the dead father replaced the young man at the cemetery, now the paternal Dracula replaces the filial Tadzio.

Bill's address to Dracula begins with some of the slangy, irreverent confidence that we heard from John at the beginning and from Bill Morris later; he calls him "sucker," a pun we might expect from John. But his prattle tapers off as the music and lights fade, "Just vamping..." (26) he explains. Of course, the word "vamping" has several meanings here. He is vamping in the musical sense, since he is merely filling in with words that have no real substance. It is a word that refers to his father's current condition. But, most importantly, we will see that he is "vamping" because he is making seductive overtures to his father. While *Death in Venice* chronicles the story of an erotic fascination with a younger man that leads to death, *A Prelude to Death in Venice* dramatizes the erotic fascination of a son with his dead father. Bill's repeated references to his father as "sucker," carry both vampiric and less exotic sexual connotations.

As Bill speaks, his tone grows less flippant. There are pauses while he listens to his father, and ellipsis marks while he thinks about what he has just heard. Both father and son experience a split between body and soul. Dracula's body seeks the darkness while his soul seeks the light; with the son, it is just the other way around. Although Bill says he's "vamping" because "we don't have a thing in common anymore" (26), it's clear that that's only what he wants to believe. As the figure of Dracula vanishes, to be replaced by a vampire bat, Bill says, "We do?" leading us to infer that Dracula has just told him what they share. Bill immediately asks for a chocolate-covered cherry to eat; earlier, he had told his father that they are just as good as drinking blood. The implication is that Bill, too, is a vampire--one of the "Undead."

The son now asks for his father's help in making the movie in Venice. He uses the language of business, "I want to incorporate in two states," but continues it in such a way that the incorporation is a commingling of identity between the father and the son, "I want to incorporate in two states--'yours' and 'mine'" (27). This 'incorporation' finds its further development in the image Bill presents from his projected Venice film:

> I'm on your lap. I'm down inside your overcoat like a kangaroo in a pocket. Well, that's my shot. Yeah, that's my point--it's a "lap" dissolve [...] I want your shoes off, and your feet in the sand, and your eyes on the water, and your hair in the fog. You know, it's Venice before the mist burns off--it's "vamping" weather. (27)

The conclusion of Mann's *Death in Venice* is restaged, with Aschenbach looking out at sea, but Tadzio is not standing out in the waves, beckoning. He is sitting on Aschenbach's lap. Carrying Bill under his overcoat, he takes the place of the mother kangaroo, figuratively "incorporating" the son within himself. The threatening and incestuous mother has completely vanished, and the father is no longer threatening.

According to the side text, a "miracle" occurs, attesting to Bill's self-proclaimed powers; "The sun appears in the night sky over the street" (27). The Dracula is restored to the (sun/son) without disaster. And the son wants to die in his father's arms; "I want to die in my father's arms looking at the sea" Bill sings to the tune of a childrens' round. The revision of Mann's story is complete: the *Liebestod* is Tadzio's, not Aschenbach's.

Bill tells the vampire bat that he will sign one of the standard contracts "in blood" (28). Longing is transferred into a knowledge, like Aschenbach's, that his desire is a transgression, but Bill is no more inclined to renounce his desire than Mann's protagonist. The desire links Eros and Thanatos in a vision of a moment of stasis (in the father's arms) that brings to an end the restlessness of artistic production. The obscene, incestuous maternal sexuality, connected with the world of the living, that puts the son--"a closet mother fucker" (15)-- to flight, and turns the father into a killer, is replaced by a delicate evocation of sexuality between a son and his maternal, deceased father. The scenario of Oedipal tragedy is transformed through Mann's homosexual romance, which substitutes male erotics for masculine rivalry. John's comic inversion of the Oedipus story finally turns out to be the plot of *A Prelude to Death in Venice*--the mother is killed, and the father is married to the son. This escape from father/son violence is no doubt what leads Bill to acknowledge his indebtedness to the author of *Death in Venice* punningly, in the play's last line, "Thanks, man..."(28), though one might well wonder whether mothers would be nearly so appreciative.

A Prelude to Death in Venice tells its story through a series a monologues. There are no sustained conversations. When Bill or Jon talk to the parents, we do not hear what the parents say. Thomas Mann, the answering machines, and the speaker from "Johns Anonymous" are oblivious to their interlocutors. Rather than developing scenes through dialectical interaction, a shifting succession of literary contexts reshapes the Actor's situation, as he moves from manic interaction with anonymous figures to a gentle longing that is focused on a single figure. The other characters, like the Actor's mother and father, are kept distant from us, and are only real insofar as they are the objects of the Actor's language. Only the facets of the Actor's character are allowed to manifest any intensity of emotion. They relay information into the circle of the Actor's perception, and are gain significance only through him. They are archetypal images, and their moment-to-moment interactions are barely represented, as one half of any conversation tends to be offstage or silent. The stage becomes a Jungian space of projections, whose interplay unfolds an interior landscape, in which all the states of affairs are not social and political, but spiritual.

CONCLUSION

All the actions in the presented world of a drama, unless otherwise subverted by the dramatist, serve to indicate the psychic states of its characters. The linguistic actions attributed to the characters, designated as the *main text*, not only manifest psychic states, but, as *expressions*, project an intentional states of affairs. Therefore, each line in the main text simultaneously serves two functions; it indicates the psychic state of the speaker and conveys information about a state of affairs. The informative function is common to most forms of discourse, but the indicative function serves a primary function in dramatic literature. The importance of this indicative function is due to the theatrical *telos* of the drama, which requires actors to speak the main text, and strengthen the indications through the physical portrayal of the character. A drama presents a dynamic interaction among the psychic states of the characters, which cannot be directly exhibited, and their external expressions in the main text. The expressions of the main text, and the *manifestative qualities* that emerge through them, modify each other as the drama develops.

The manifestative qualities in an expression are conveyed through a number of devices, which serve to limit the valid range of interpretations by an actor. The devices include: punctuation, word choice, word order, and imagery. The use of punctuation can strongly indicate the emotional quality of a line, as well as clarify syntax and word order. Thomas Bernhard's decision to avoid punctuation limits the range of his dramatic language. Grammatically well-formed sentences, parallel constructions, abstractions, and sentences with clear and complex schemes of syntactical subordination tend to manifest less intense qualities, and, in its purest form, are used to characterize practical, rational, and characters who seem more intellectually than emotionally centered, such as Combe in *Bingo* or Koerber-Kent in *The Irrational Are Dying out*. Intense emotions that tend to break down the rational processes of thought are often manifested through sentence fragments, interjections, syntactical ambiguities, concrete images, superlatives, and hyperbole. Such devices as these tend to define the level of intensity, rather than any specific emotion.

Characters whose semantic contexts vary little from speech to speech, like the Writer in *The Hunting Party*, tend to reveal obsessiveness or dogmatism. The limited context of their language also tends to limit them to a narrowly circumscribed range of emotion. Such characters have highly *monologic* contexts. Even the dialogic interaction in a play may strongly assert a single context, as in *The Hunting Party*. When the characters tend to share a single linguistic context (*The Hunting Party, Véra Baxter*), the play tends more toward the lyrical state, since we feel the voices of the characters being subsumed within the language of the presenter. In plays in which the characters' language is more highly differentiated (*Bingo, Inadmissible Evidence*), the presence of the presenter is minimized, and the dramatic elements are strengthened.

Characters who repeatedly modify their own linguistic contexts, elaborating and modifying their states of affairs through different voices within themselves, such as Bill Maitland in *Inadmissible Evidence*, tend to show a higher degree of intellectual sophistication, emotional complexity, psychic fragmentation, or doubt, than those with a single, monolithic language. Even the monologues of such characters may be composed of strongly diverse means of expression, or *dialogization of monologue*. Through this device, the dramatist can manifest emotional tensions through the warring linguistic contexts of a single character. This device is taken to an extreme in a work like *A Prelude to Death in Venice*, in which a single performer plays a succession of characters, each of which represents a distinct and separate facet of a single psyche.

Further emotional qualities emerge through the interaction of speakers. The speeches may be linked primarily on the linguistic level, in which case the subject matter tends to predominate, and the speeches tend to explain or elaborate upon the topic. The linguistic links testify to the presence of a shared vocabulary, since many words used by one speaker will tend to appear in the speeches of the other speakers as well. If the emotional intensity of this kind of dialogue is low, it will tend to be a *conversation*, in which the manifestative qualities are subordinated to the truth claims of the topic. If the exchange is more intense, it will tend toward the *dispute*, in which the speakers use language to define themselves in opposition to each other. Stichomythia, for example, is distinguished by a great number of linguistic links, a sharply defined contrast between the speakers and their values, and a strong tendency toward disputation, whether in a comic or melodramatic mode.

If the linguistic links are few, the dialogue tends to be unified in its extralinguistic situation. In that case, the terms of the opposition are less sharply defined, or even non-existent, and the characters lack common concerns. Tensions are then generated by the way characters avoid directly responding to each other, as the General's Wife ignores the Writer's revelations in the opening scene of *The Hunting Party* or as Véra and Monique Combes carefully avoid confrontation in *Véra Baxter*.

As linguistic links lessen, the use of pauses and extended silences becomes a more common device. Dramatic silences can indicate a great range of emotions, from indifference to deadly antagonism, but they only become meaningful insofar as the main text defines the significance of the silence. Shakespeare's silences in *Bingo*, for example, are defined through the antagonism they provoke, as well as by the attitudes Shakespeare manifests when he speaks. In *Véra Baxter*, Marguerite Duras establishes and maintains ambiguities by the frequent use of pauses that are not clearly defined by the main text, but point to the mysteriousness of her characters and the situations they find themselves in. These uses of silence help to differentiate dramatic literature from other theatrical forms. In pantomime, where there is only silence, the silence is defined through the conventions of the form. In musical theatre, instrumental music shapes the pauses between main text far more specifically than dramatic texts ever can.

The manifestative qualities are not, however, the only affective qualities that appear within a text. The speeches of the Writer and Shakespeare are not always rich in manifestative qualities, but are often rich in other affective qualities because of the emotional power of the situation that is projected through their states of affairs. The bear-baiting speech in *Bingo* becomes shocking by virtue of the scene it describes; the Writer's litany of the omnipresence of Death in *The Hunting Party* makes a strong statement through its repetitions and the extremes through which it states its argument. Speech can also gain strength through its interaction with the visual elements specified in the side text; the picnic before the gallows in *Bingo*, or the bizarre metamorphosis of Quitt's apartment in the second part of *The Irrational Are Dying out*. In both cases the manifestative qualities interact with, and are colored by, the affective qualities that simultaneously emerge from the setting, and the states of affairs that are projected through the main text.

The dynamic relationship between the main text, the physical setting, and the dramatic situation is highly fluid, and the dominant aspect changes frequently, even in the course of a single scene. All three aspects, however, exist simultaneously, and are perceived as a configuration. The third scene of *Bingo* juxtaposes a pleasant afternoon with a body on a gibbet (side text), and Shakespeare's isolation (side text) with the good humor of the workers (main text). The primary affective quality emerges from the interaction of all these elements, even though one of them may take primary attention at any given moment.

Furthermore, the affective quality of any given moment is not perceived independently of the moments that preceded it. Each moment is influenced by everything that has happened in the text up to then. Véra Baxter's scream over the telephone is given weight by the emotional understatement that has been maintained up to that point.

In the course of a drama, a dialectical relationship unfolds between the extralinguistic situation and the main text. The extralinguistic situation is composed both of the physical setting and the dramatic situation at that moment. The reciprocal modification of the main text and the dramatic situation is particularly apparent in *active speech*, a form particularly congenial to dramatic language. There, the characters use language to move their interlocutors toward certain ends, as Jonson first tries to cajole and then provoke Shakespeare into revealing his writing plans, or as Maitland tries to keep Hudson and his other fellow workers from deserting him. In such cases, the conflict between various objectives heightens the level of manifestative qualities, as the characters meet with resistance from each other. Objectives manifest themselves in active speech, altering both the linguistic and extralinguistic contexts. In *The Hunting Party*, where many of the speeches elaborate theme without developing conflict, the text runs the peril of failing to exhibit a sufficiently varied range of affective qualities. A similar problem can be seen in *Véra Baxter*, in which the language often tends to serve the primary function of cloaking emotion or rendering it ambiguous. There, the active quality of the discourse is often muted.

The impulse toward emotional variety is countered by the unifying structure of the work, which predominantly functions through a plot that develops through the interacting objectives of the characters, a dominant mood or atmosphere, or thematic structure. When this unity is achieved, the drama is no longer a mere string of emotions intuited by the spectator in turn, but becomes a highly sophisticated configuration, in which all the elements contribute to the intuition of a complex quality (Ingarden 1973 *Literary Work*, 293-295; 1973 *Cognition,* 62). Although the drama is experienced in its moment-to-moment unfolding, the entire play can be perceived by the spectator as a unified structure that engenders its own unique emotional configuration. This perception most commonly occurs at the end of the play, when the spectator can constitute the succession of moments into a whole, or at the climaxes of the work, where lines of plot, imagery, motif and atmosphere culminate.

The six plays in this study share certain qualities, yet they develop them differently. They all share an elegiac and alienated tone, which is a function of the alienation and tendency toward silence in each of the protagonists. Direct and extended disputes are rare, and silences underscore the psychological distances among the characters in all of them. In *Inadmissible Evidence*, the manifestative qualities of Maitland dominate, engendering strong empathic involvement with him. In *Bingo*, the protagonist is viewed with greater objectivity and criticism. His dominant qualities are coldness, despondency, self-pity, and hatred, which emerge through his sparse language, frequent silences, and brooding monologues. His inability to enunciate his new-found insights as active language and thus influence others leads to affective qualities of frustration and despair. The educational movement of the play finally appears as aborted and incomplete. *Véra Baxter* reverses that process. There, the isolated protagonist finally finds an interlocutor who helps her in the telling of her story, and takes an initial step toward overcoming her near-tragic isolation.

The next three plays move even further away from realism, and the presented worlds are more strongly dominated by protagonists who remain surprisingly unaffected by other characters. In *The Hunting Party*, the most loquacious character does not change, and the only character who does change, the General, does not ever oppose his destruction at the hands of the Writer; indeed, he may even invite it. The manifestative qualities of individual characters are subordinated to a lyric vision of death that is articulated by the Writer. In *The Irrational are Dying out*, the play develops through the clash of subworlds. As Quitt moves progressively away from the world of rationality, his quest gains in expressiveness, but increasingly loses intersubjective meaning. At the end, we are left with only an inchoate landscape of diverse objects. Finally, in *A Prelude to Death in Venice*, we have a psychological drama, in which we see no one but the facets of a single character, with the outside world reduced to the most schematic of images. A causal plot line is replaced by a succession of archetypes--a sort of Jungian masque.

Although the dispute is the form of language most inherently dramatic, these plays tend to avoid it, and experiment with other ways to manifest and develop psychic states on stage. Since all of these plays take alienation as a given, the direct confrontation of opposing forces implicit in the dispute is an inappropriate form for them. As a result, the protagonists tend to indulge in monologues, with the exception of Véra, whose very incapacity to monologize is seen as part of her problem. Even in *The Irrational Are Dying out*, which opposes two realms of discourse, the realms by definition cannot sustain interaction, and any dialectical development is impossible.

All of these playwrights are to various degrees the heirs of Anton Chekhov. Rejecting the intense interaction, relentless causality, dialectical development and linguistically homogeneous reality that tended to dominate the European stage from the Enlightenment through the realistic dramas of Ibsen, Chekhov explored alternative means of developing and manifesting emotional qualities in his dramas that paved the way for these six playwrights. Tensions are manifested less by confrontations than by evasion or retreat. The main text tends to be characterized by disjunction, and tends to be unified on the extralinguistic level instead of the linguistic. Following Chekhov, all of these dramatists start with a premise of fragmentation, which takes them away from the techniques to the well-made play to experiment with other, often more lyrical, devices.

Rationally explicable relationships grow rarer and rarer, as we move from Osborne to Breuer. Key images tend to be composed of unmediated juxtapositions; music in *The Hunting Party*, the Old Lady's reminiscence in *Bingo*, the novella by Stifter in *The Irrational are Dying out*, the Stranger's tale of the medieval Véra in *Véra Baxter*, a message from Thomas Mann interrupting the Oedipal crisis of *A Prelude to Death in Venice*, the 'inadmissible' parts of every testimony in Osborne's play. Each exists incongruously, even miraculously, in their presented world. These gentle, aesthetically pleasing moments are granted to their characters as moments of grace that defy any rational foundation in their worlds. Alienation is the iron law, and the brief interludes in which the suffering of life is suspended through memory, art, imagination or love resists explanation according to that iron law. No dialectical relationship can lead from misery to these privileged moments.

In an intriguing essay, Hoffmeister (1987) has argued that post-modern playwrights, such as Handke, Bernhard, and Botho Strauß, gain much of their power and distinctiveness by deconstructing those very elements of the theatre that have constituted its power--including the illusions of individuality, of a stable past, of a political structure, and a literary tradition. Theatre is replaced by pastiche, with a resultant loss of aura. She ends with the ominous prediction

> When deconstruction is enacted on the stage, I contend that the dying of all traditions, both articulated and accentuated by post-modern theater, may contribute to the dying of theater as such. We all know that theater attendance has drastically declined in recent years. (Hoffmeister, 437)

The movement from Osborne to Breuer, charted through these plays, may lead to a similar conclusion. As contemporary playwrights move farther from those elements of dramatically active speech, conflict, and character interaction that found the aesthetic strengths of the art form, we are presented with plays that are ingenious, striking and even moving, but which relegate themselves to being minor statments because they tend to avoid what the form does best. For all of their virtues, and there are many, it is important to note that none of these plays have firmly established themselves in the repertoires of the Western theatre, and their obscurity is likely to increase in the coming years. True to a vision of life that is increasingly undramatic, the playwrights from Osborne to Breuer enrich our awareness of new expressive potentials at the peripheries of drama, but leave the center empty.

WORKS CITED

Primary Sources

Bernhard, Thomas. *Der Atem*. Salzburg: Residenz, 1978.

———. *Die Jagdgesellschaft*. Frankfurt am Main: Suhrkamp, 1975.

———. *Die Macht der Gewohnheit. Die Salzburger Stücke*. Frankfurt am Main: Suhrkamp, 1975: 97-197.

Bond, Edward. *"Bingo" and "The Sea."* New York: Hill & Wang, 1975.

———. *"The Fool" and "We Come to the River."* London: Eyre Methuen, 1976.

———. *Lear*. New York: Hill & Wang, 1972.

———. *Saved*. New York: Hill & Wang, 1965.

Breuer, Lee. *A Prelude to Death in Venice. New Plays USA 1*. Edited by James Leverett. New York: Theatre Communications Group, 1982: 11-28.

Dickens, Charles. *Works*. New York: Avenal, 1978.

Duras, Marguerite. *Véra Baxter, or The Atlantic Beaches*. Translated by Philippa Wehle. *Dramacontemporary: France*. Edited by Philippa Wehle. New York: PAJ Publications, 1986: 19-41.

———. *Véra Baxter, ou les Plages de Atlantique*. Paris: Éditions Albatros, 1980.

Handke, Peter. *Der kurze Brief zum langen Abschied*. Frankfurt am Main: Suhrkamp, 1975.

———. *Die Unvernünftigen sterben aus*. Frankfurt am Main: Suhrkamp, 1973.

———. *They Are Dying Out. The Ride Across Lake Constance and Other Plays*. Translated by Michael Roloff, in collaboration with Karl Weber. New York: Farrar, Straus & Giroux, 1976: 165-258.

James, Henry. *Novels, 1871-1830*. Edited by William T. Stafford. New York: Literary Classics of U.S., 1983.

Lyly, John. *Complete Works*. Edited by R. Warwick Bond. Oxford: Clarendon Press, 1902.

Mann, Thomas. "Der Tod in Venedig". *Die Erzählungen. Fiorenza. Gesang vom Kindchen. Gedichte.* Oldenburg: S. Fischer, 1966: 444-525.

Osborne, John. *Inadmissible Evidence: A Play*. New York: Grove Press, 1965.

Pinter, Harold. *"The Lover," "Tea Party," "The Basement"*. New York: Grove Press, 1967.

Shakespeare, William. *Titus Andronicus*. Edited by J. C. Maxwell. Cambridge, Mass.: Harvard University Press, 1953.

Shaw, George Bernard. *The Doctor's Dilemma: A Tragedy*. Baltimore: Penguin, 1954.

Sophocles. *Oedipus the King*. Translated by Stephen Berg & Diskin Clay. New York: Oxford University Press, 1978.

Webster, John. *The Duchess of Malfi*. Edited by Clive Hart. Edinburgh: Oliver & Boyd, 1972.

Critical Sources

Archer, William. *Play-Making*. London: Chapman, 1913.

Aristotle. *Ethica Nichomachea*. Translated by W. D. Ross. Vol. 9, *Works*. Oxford: Clarendon Press, 1925.

Artaud, Antonin. *The Theatre and Its Double*. Translated by Mary C. Richards. New York: Grove Press, 1958.

Bakhtin, Mikhail. *Problems of Dostoyevsky's Poetics*. Translated by W. Ratsel.[N.P.]: Ardis, 1973.

Barnham, Martin. *Osborne*. Edinburgh: Oliver and Boyd, 1969.

Barthes, Roland. *S/Z*. Translated by Richard Miller. New York: Hill & Wang, 1974.

Blank, Richard. *Sprache und Dramaturgie: Die Aischyleische Kassandraszene, das Osterspiel von Klosterneuberg, Machiavelli's "Mandragola."* München: Wilhelm Fink, 1969.

Blumer, Arnold. Peter Handke's romantische Unvernunft. *Acta Germanica*. 8 (1973): 123-32.

Brecht, Bertolt. *Gesammelte Werke*. v.16. Frankfurt am Main: Suhrkamp, 1967.

Brook, Peter. *The Empty Space*. New York: Atheneum, 1969.

Brown, Charles T. & Charles van Riper. *Speech and Man*. Englewood Cliffs: Prentice-Hall, 1966.

Brown, John Russell. *Theatre Language: A Study of Arden, Osborne, Pinter, and Wesker*. London: Allen Lane, 1972.

_____. *Theatre Language: A Study of Arden, Osborne, Pinter and Wesker*. London: Allen Lane, 1972.

Bulman, James C. Bond, Shakespeare, and the Absurd. *Modern Drama*. 29 (March 1986): 343-354.

Carter, Alan. *John Osborne*. Edinburgh: Oliver and Boyd, 1969.

Chambers, Helen. Theatre Checklist No. 12: Thomas Bernhard. *Theatrefacts* 3 (1976): 3-11.

Cody, Gabrielle. Love in the Durassian World: An Introduction to *Agatha*. *Theater* 20, 1 (Winter 1988-89): 18-21.

Cohn, Ruby. The Fabulous Theatre of Edward Bond. *Essays on Contemporary British Drama*. Edited by Hedvig Bock and Albert Wertheim. München: Max Hueber, 1981.

Dauenhauer, Bernard P. On Silence. *Research in Phenomenology* 3 (1973): 9-27.

_____. Silence. An Intentional Analysis. *Research in Phenomenology* 6 (1976): 63-83.

Durbach, Errol. Herod in the Welfare State: *Kindermord* in the Plays of Edward Bond. *Educational Theatre Journal* 27 (December 1975): 482-487.

Eisner, Nicholas. *Theatertheater/Theaterspiele*: The Plays of Thomas Bernhard. *Modern Drama* 30 (March 1987): 104-114.

Elam, Keir. *The Semiotics of Theatre and Drama*. London: Methuen, 1980.

Eliopulos, James. *Samuel Beckett's Dramatic Language*. The Hague: Mouton,

Ellis-Fermor, Una. *The Frontiers of Drama*. Second Edition. London: Methuen, 1961.

Esslin, Martin. *The Field of Drama: How the Signs of Drama Create Meaning on Stage and Screen*. London: Methuen, 1987.

_____. *The Theatre of the Absurd*. Garden City: Anchor, 1961.

Falk, Eugene H. *The Poetics of Roman Ingarden*. Chapel Hill: University of North Carolina, 1981.

_____. *Types of Thematic Structure: The Nature and Function of Motifs in Gide, Camus, and Sartre*. Introduction by Bernard Weinberg. Chicago: University of Chicago Press, 1967.

Freytag, Gustav. *Techniques of the Drama*. Translated by Elias J. MacEwan. New York: Benjamin Blom, 1968.

Gadamer, Hans-Georg. *Philosophical Hermeneutics*. Translated by David E. Linge. Berkeley: University of California Press, 1976.

_____. *Truth and Method*. Translated by Garrett Barden & William Glendoepel. New York : Seabury Press, 1975.

Gampers, Herbert. *Thomas Bernhard*. München: Deutscher Taschenbuch Verlag, 1977.

Gilman, Richard. *The Making of Modern Drama: A Study of Büchner, Ibsen, Strindberg, Chekhove, Pirandello, Brecht, Beckett, Handke*. New York: Farrar, Straus & Giroux, 1974.

Gross, Robert F. "The Greatest Uncertainty": The Perils of Performance in Thomas Bernhard's *Der Ignorant und der Wahnsinnige*. *Modern Drama* 23, 4 (August 1980): 365-380.

Grotowski, Jerzy. *Towards a Poor Theatre*. New York: Simon and Schuster, 1968.

Gusdorf, Georges. *Speaking*. Translated by Paul T. Brockelman. Evanston: Northwestern University Press, 1965.

Guthrie, Sir Tyrone. An Audience of One. *Modern Culture and the Art*. Edited by James B. Hall and Barry Ulanov. New York: McGraw-Hill, 1967: 368-79.

Handke, Peter. Horváth ist besser. *Theater Heute* 3 (March 1968), 28.

Hay, Malcolm & Philip Roberts. *Bond: A Study of His Plays*. London: Eyre Methuen, 1980.

Hayes, Tom & Lee Quinby. The Aporia of Bourgeois Art: Desire in Thomas Mann's *Death in Venice*. *Criticism* 31, 2 (Spring 1989): 159-178.

Hayman, Ronald, *John Osborne*. New York : Frederick Ungar, 1972.

Heller, Erich. *Thomas Mann: The Ironic German*. Cleveland: Meridian, 1961.

Hoffmeister, Donna L. Post-modern Theatre: A Contradiction in Terms? *Monatshefte* 79, 4 (Winter, 1987): 424-438.

Husserl, Edmund. *Cartesian Meditations: An Introduction to Phenomenology*. Translated by Doris Cairns. The Hague: Martinus Nijhoff, 1960.

_____. *Logical Investigations*. Translated by J. N. Findlay. London: Routledge and Kegan Paul, 1970.

Ingarden, Roman. *The Cognition of the Literary Work of Art*. Translated by Ruth Ann Crowley and Kenneth R. Olson. Evanston: Northwestern University Press, 1973.

―――. *The Literary Work of Art: An Investigation on the Borderlines of Ontology, Logic, and the Theory of Literature*. Translated by George C. Grabowicz. Evanston: Northwestern University Press, 1973.

Johnson, Mary J. Verbal and Non-Verbal Communication in the Theatre of Marguerite Duras: A Thematic and Semiotic Study. Ph.D. diss., University of Wisconsin-Madison, 1987.

Jurgensen, Manfred. Die Sprachpartituren des Thomas Bernhard. *Bernhard: Annäherungen*. Edited by Manfred Jurgensen. Bern: Franck, 1981: 99-122.

Kennedy, Andrew W. *Six Dramatists in Search of a Language: Studies in Dramatic Language*. Cambridge: Cambridge University Press, 1975.

Klotz, Volker. *Gesclossene und Offene Form im Drama*. München: Carl Hanser, 1969.

Lehrman, Wolfgang. *Lyrik Epik Dramatik. Die totgesagte Trinität*. Meisenheim: Anton Hain, 1973.

Mander, Gertrud. Die Goya-Welt des Edward Bonds. *Theater Heute* 10 (May 1969): 37-38.

Mann, Bruce J. O'Neill's "Presence" in *Long Day's Journey Into Night*. *The Theatre Annual* 1988, 15-30.

Marranca, Bonnie, ed. *The Theatre of Images*. New York: Drama Book Specialists, 1977.

―――. The Self as Text: Uses of Autobiography in the Theatre (*Animations* as Model). *Performing Arts Journal* 4 (1979): 85-105.

Moore, Sonia. *The Stanislavski System*. New York: Viking, 1965.

Mukařovský, Jan. *The Word and Verbal Art: Selected Essays*. Translated by John Burbank and Peter Steiner. New Haven: Yale University Press, 1977.

Nägele, Reinar & Renate Voris. *Peter Handke*. München: Beck, 1978.

Ohmann, Richard. *Shaw: The Style and the Man*. Middletown: Wesleyan University Press, 1962.

Papin, Liliane. *L'autre scène: Le théâtre de Marguerite Duras*. Saratoga, Calif.: Anma Libri, 1988.

Peymann, Claus. Thomas Bernhard auf der Bühne. *Literarisches Kolloquium 1984: Thomas Bernhard. Materialien*. Edited by Alfred Pittertschatscher & Johann Lachinger. Linz: Land Oberösterreich, 1985: 190-192.

Prior, Moody. *The Language of Tragedy*. Bloomington: Indiana University Press, 1947.

Quiqley, Austin. *The Pinter Problem*. Princeton: Princeton University Press, 1975.

Reed, T. J. *Thomas Mann: The Uses of Tradition*. Oxford: Clarendon Press, 1974.

Riesman, David. *The Lonely Crowd: A Study of the Changing American Character*. With Nathan Glazer & Reuel Denney. Abridged by authors. Garden City: Doubleday, 1953.

Schlueter, June. Politics and Poetry: Peter Handke's *They Are Dying Out*. Modern Drama 23, 4 (Jan. 1981): 339-45.

Schopenhauer, Arthur. *The World as Will and Idea*. Translated by R. Burton Haldane & J. Kamp. London: Kegan Paul, Trench, Trubner, 1891.

Staiger, Emil. *Grundbegriffe der Poetik*. Zürich: Atlantis, 1956.

Stanislavski, Konstantin. *An Actor Prepares*. Translated by Elizabeth Hapgood. New York : Theatre Arts, 1936,

States, Bert O. *Irony and Drama: A Poetics*. Ithaca: Cornell University Press, 1971.

Stern, Daniel N. On Kinesic Analysis. *The Drama Review*, 17 (1973): 114-131.

Stoll. Karlheinz. *Harold Pinter. Ein Beitrag zur Typologie des neuen englischen Dramas*. Düsseldorf: August Basel, 1977.

Szondi, Peter. *Theorie des modernen Dramas (1880-1950)*. Frankfurt am Main: Suhrkamp, 1978.

Trussler, Simon. *The Plays of John Osborne*. London: Victor Gallancz, 1969.

Veltruský, Jiři. Basic Features of Dramatic Dialogue. *Semiotics of Art: Prague School Contributions*. Edited by Ladislav Matejka & Irwin R. Titunik. Cambridge, Mass.: MIT Press, 1976: 128-133.

———. Construction of Semantic Contexts. *Semiotics of Art: Prague School Contributions*. Edited by Ladislav Matejka & Irwin R. Titunik. Cambridge, Mass.: MIT Press, 1976: 134-44.

———. Dramatic Text as a Component of Theatre. *Semiotics of Art: Prague School Contributions*. Edited by Ladislav Matejka & Irwin R. Titunik. Cambridge, Mass.: MIT Press, 1976: 94-117.

Willis, Sharon A. *Marguerite Duras: Writing on the Body*. Urbana: University of Illinois Press, 1987.

———. Staging Sexual Difference: Reading, Recitation, and Repetition in Duras' *Malady of Death*. *Feminine Focus: the New Women Playwrights*. Edited by Enoch Brater. Oxford: Oxford University Press, 1989: 109-125.

Wise, Jennifer. Marginalizing Drama: Bakhtin's Theory of Genre. *Essays in Theatre*. 8, 1 (Nov. 1989): 15-22.

Wolfensperger, Peter. *Edward Bond: Dialektik des Weltbildes und dramatische Gestaltung*. Bonn: Francke, 1976.

Worth, Katharine J. Edward Bond. *Essays on Contemporary British Drama*. Edited by Hedwig Bock and Albert Wertheim. München: Max Hueber, 1981: 205-222.

Worthen, John. Endings and Beginnings: Edward Bond and the Shock of Recognition? *Educational Theatre Journal* 27 (December 1975): 466-479.